Markets

IN SEARCH OF MEDIA

Götz Bachmann, Timon Beyes, Mercedes Bunz,
and Wendy Hui Kyong Chun, Series Editors

Pattern Discrimination
Markets
Communication
Machine
Remain

Markets

Armin Beverungen, Philip Mirowski, Edward Nik-Khah, and Jens Schröter

IN SEARCH OF MEDIA

University of Minnesota Press
Minneapolis
London

meson press

In Search of Media is a collaboration between the
University of Minnesota Press and meson press,
an open access publisher, https://meson.press/.

Published by the
University of Minnesota Press, 2019
111 Third Avenue South, Suite 290
Minneapolis, MN 55401-2520
https://www.upress.umn.edu

in collaboration with
meson press
Salzstrasse 1
21335 Lüneburg, Germany
https://meson.press

ISBN 978-1-5179-0646-7 (pb)
A Cataloging-in-Publication record for this book is available
from the Library of Congress.

The University of Minnesota is an equal-opportunity educator
and employer.

UMP BmB

Contents

Series Foreword

"Media determine our situation," Friedrich Kittler infamously wrote in his Introduction to *Gramophone, Film, Typewriter.* Although this dictum is certainly extreme—and media archaeology has been critiqued for being overly dramatic and focused on technological developments—it propels us to keep thinking about media as setting the terms for which we live, socialize, communicate, organize, do scholarship, et cetera. After all, as Kittler continued in his opening statement almost thirty years ago, our situation, "in spite or because" of media, "deserves a description." What, then, are the terms—the limits, the conditions, the periods, the relations, the phrases—of media? And, what is the relationship between these terms and determination? This book series, *In Search of Media,* answers these questions by investigating the often elliptical "terms of media" under which users operate. That is, rather than produce a series of explanatory keyword-based texts to describe media practices, the goal is to understand the conditions (the "terms") under which media is produced, as well as the ways in which media impacts and changes these terms.

Clearly, the rise of search engines has fostered the proliferation and predominance of keywords and terms. At the same time, it has changed the very nature of keywords, since now any word and pattern can become "key." Even further, it has transformed the very process of learning, since search presumes that, (a) with the right phrase, any question can be answered and (b) that the answers lie within the database. The truth, in other words, is "in there." The impact of search/media on knowledge, however, goes beyond search engines. Increasingly, disciplines—from sociology to economics, from the arts to literature—are in search of media as a way to revitalize their methods and objects of study. Our current media situation therefore seems to imply a new term, understood as temporal shifts of mediatic conditioning. Most broadly, then, this series asks: What are the terms or conditions of knowledge itself?

To answer this question, each book features interventions by two (or more) authors, whose approach to a term—to begin with: *communication, pattern discrimination, markets, remain, machine*—diverge and converge in surprising ways. By pairing up scholars from North America and Europe, this series also advances media theory by obviating the proverbial "ten year gap" that exists across language barriers due to the vagaries of translation and local academic customs. The series aims to provoke new descriptions, prescriptions, and hypotheses—to rethink and reimagine what media can and must do.

[1]

Capital's Media

Armin Beverungen

Why search for media in markets? The other contributions to this book provide two answers. One answer is that markets, at least for neoliberal economists, have for a long time been understood as information-processing machines and are designed—also on the basis of a number of digital media technologies—with that function in mind. Moreover, the political and cultural program of neoliberalism has sought to reconfigure states, organizations, subjects, and their relations in the image of "the market" at least since the 1980s.[1] One question for media theory that follows is whether we want to become handmaidens of engineering economists designing markets, to find ways of designing markets differently, or to design other media for a different kind of relationality. Another answer is that in markets we find money as a prerequisite medium, one that provides the general equivalent by which commodities can be exchanged. Money points us beyond markets, since as a medium it determines our situation and precedes other media, and it points to capital accumulation, which depends on it and which is historically shaped by different kinds of money. One question for media theory here becomes whether we want to provide a media archaeology of money, or get involved in building alternative currencies or forms of exchange and equivalence.

To situate the other contributions contained in this book within a media theory of markets, which is very much yet to come, we will refer to a number of debates and works that one could count and enroll in the project. To begin, however, it might be worth briefly to consider what kind of media theory of markets is not offered here, and why. To do so, let's start at the so-called end of history, if only because the only thing that was said to survive this end was the market; or, rather, everything that was to exist was expected to pass through the market.[2]

The Market as Invisible Hand and Site of Truth

In an essay on postmodernism and the market contained in his book on the cultural logic of late capitalism, Fredric Jameson famously rallied his readers against the rhetoric and ideology of the market promoted by neoliberal economists, since the "surrender to the various forms of market ideology on the left . . . not to mention everybody else has been imperceptible but alarmingly universal" (1991, 263). Jameson asserted: "'The market is in human nature' is the proposition that cannot be allowed to stand unchallenged; in my opinion, it is the most crucial terrain of ideological struggle in our time" (1991, 263–64). Among other things, Jameson speculates on why markets have become so popular, which he finds astonishing: "namely, how the dreariness of business and private property, the dustiness of entrepreneurship, and the well-nigh Dickensian flavor of title and appropriation, coupon-clipping, mergers, investment banking, and other such transactions . . . should in our time have proved to be so *sexy*" (1991, 274, emphasis in original).

The answer for Jameson resides in the "illicit metaphorical association" of the market with "the media itself in its largest contemporary and global sense (including an infrastructure of all the latest media gadgets and high technology)," wherein "two systems of codes are identified in such a way as to allow the libidinal energies of the one to suffuse the other" (1991, 275). Jameson suggests that this operation takes place in three steps: the commodities produced for the market also populate our television screens; technological gadgets promising the end of class provide a pleasure that is manifest and celebrated in media consumption; and finally, media content itself is commodified and marketed, so that market and media ultimately become indistinguishable (1991, 275–77). Jameson here, in a cultural Marxist register, speculates on a media theory of markets whose principal task is to provide a critique of the ideology of the market at the level of representation, with media primarily playing the role of legitimating the market through associating it with *jouissance.*

This is not exactly the media theory of markets on offer here, since, at least for Philip Mirowski, it deals with less than half of the story that needs to be told when it comes to the rise and dominance of neoliberal exhortations of the market. As Mirowski has extensively argued elsewhere (2013), a key difference between classic liberal economists and neoliberal economists is that the latter no longer deem markets to be natural. Instead, neoliberals have, since at least the 1980s, been in the business of constructing markets, and this is where we need to direct our attention also, as media theorists, as digital media technologies are intimately enrolled in this project. Jameson, therefore, at least if we follow Mirowski, mischaracterizes neoliberalism and thereby misconstrues the political task at hand. The claim that markets are natural still gets made by members of the Neoliberal Thought Collective, but only as part of its "double-truth doctrine" (Mirowski 2013, 68–83): the exoteric version of this doctrine—directed at nonmembers of the collective—upholds the claim that the market constitutes a spontaneous, natural order of exchange; the esoteric version—directed at members of the collective—quite happily admits that markets should be designed and constructed.

Nonetheless, a media theory of markets might want to ask how the exoteric part of the double-truth doctrine of neoliberalism functions. How is it that markets are framed for us (assuming we are not part of the Neoliberal Thought Collective), if not as natural or spontaneous then as harbingers of truth? How is it that the market gains authority over practically every realm of life, as something God-like, most famously through the figure of the "invisible hand"? And how, if the market is said to offer truth, does it speak? Campbell Jones has, in a deconstructive, psychoanalytic register, explored the ascription of personhood and speech to markets. For Jones, to "imagine that something like the market is a kind of person that has a will, intentions and might speak" is "a shared or collective psychosis in which two or more share a common delusion" (Jones 2013, 20). What is particular about how the market speaks to us is its structural similarity to God, where the market is turned into "an imagined external agent with special powers" (17). Much like God, the market mumbles, as Jones puts it, and the speaking subject that is the market "involves a fundamental and almost permanent mystery as to which intending subject might lie behind the speech of the market and animate it" (38).

Although Jones focuses on the metaphysical and abstract features of markets and their political consequences, a media theory of markets might want to ask, with Jones, how precisely the market speaks, and how its speech is mediated. While the market appears largely supersensual, Jones already notes that to participate in markets "often involves a radical overstimulation of the senses": "It is not that the market does not surround us with sounds, but rather what to do with these sounds and how to understand what it means to listen to them" (20). Jones's focus on sound partially derives from one case where he engages with the media of markets, specifically the TickTrola,[3] a software that turns financial market signals into music. Yet there is certainly a plethora of media of markets, some of which we will discuss below in relation to high-frequency trading.[4] For contemporary media theory, it will certainly not come as a surprise that markets are as little disenchanted as media, that media might be at work in conjuring spirits (Geoghegan 2016), or that markets involve a certain spectrality (Vogl 2015). So, media theory might want to turn its analytical capacities toward the media of markets that sustain its speech, personhood, and spirituality.

One key consideration here will be to what extent a Foucauldian register may be built upon in this vein. The publication and subsequent translation of Michel Foucault's lectures on the birth of biopolitics have been central to a renewed analysis of neoliberalism and the way it establishes the market as a "site of veridiction" (Foucault 2008, 30–37). Yet, as Mirowski (2013) and Wendy Brown (2015, 54) have noted, Foucault does not sufficiently distinguish between liberalism and neoliberalism. This is politically counterproductive, since it associates neoliberalism with *laissez faire* or the deregulation of markets. Joseph Vogl—to take a key figure in German media and cultural studies writing in a Foucauldian register—in *The Specters of Capital* focuses in much detail on the figure of the invisible hand (2015, 23–27 and throughout)—a liberal metaphor associated with *laissez faire.* Even as Vogl considers the importance of economic theory (specifically Black-Scholes) for the design of markets (2015, 72–74), and discusses the media of markets in terms of the coincidence of the expansion of derivative trading with computing history and information technology (2015, 75), this approach seems to foreclose a more careful engagement with the constructive side of neoliberalism.

For the exoteric part of the double-truth doctrine of the neoliberals, i.e. that part directed at nonmembers of the Neoliberal Thought Collective, what is more important than portraying the market as governed by an invisible hand is to claim it as a site of truth. In Mirowski's view, Foucault and many who follow him take this part of the neoliberal doctrine too much at face value: the crucial feature to note is that the governmentality construed by the neoliberals "elevates the market as a site of truth *for everyone but themselves*" (2013, 98; emphasis in original). This is why much of Foucauldian scholarship on the market in neoliberalism has disregarded the other side of the double-truth doctrine—namely, how neoliberals construct markets. Neoliberals are seen as politicians reforming the state, not as economists reconstructing markets. In this way, Ute Tellmann notes, "economy never becomes an object of analysis in its own right; therefore the mediation of relations of power through money and objects drops from view" (2009, 8). The invisible hand here serves to defy "the forms of critical visibility commonly associated with Foucault's work," and the "invisibility of the market is directed against the very analytical perspective Foucault typically assumes, one aimed at detecting the instruments, positions, and architectures that produce such epistemological claims and privileges" (2009, 22).

Tellmann therefore calls for a "more typical Foucauldian approach" (22) to counteract this blindness. One might wonder also whether other strands of contemporary media theory working, for example, with a Kittlerian reading of Foucault could contribute to this endeavor. Notwithstanding the reasons for the scarcity of such literature (outlined by Schröter in this book), Ralph and Stefan Heidenreich's book on money as a *dispositif* of power, even if only loosely associated with this tradition, might be one contribution (Heidenreich and Heidenreich 2008).

Neoliberal Engineering and Market Design

This is where Mirowski's work with Edward Nik-Khah here and in their book entitled *The Knowledge We Have Lost in Information* (2017) comes in. In their contribution to this volume, Nik-Khah and Mirowski unravel the "deep history" of Friedrich Hayek's impact on the economics profession, in particular the way in which his views on information in markets correspond to key precepts of emerging approaches to market design. In so doing, our authors contend that despite the economists' version of history in which Hayek has hardly been influential in orthodox economics, "neoliberalism has occupied the profession's heartland, and has planted its flag." While Nik-Khah and Mirowski show how market design is "the unintended consequence of orthodox economists grappling with themes introduced by Hayek," today market design "constitutes the precepts of neoliberalism taken to their logical conclusion." It is not simply the market as governed by an invisible hand, but the market as an "*omnipotent* processor of information" (emphasis in original), which justifies the reorganization of the economic lifeworld on the basis of markets.

Around a decade ago, Mirowski had suggested that a key challenge for intellectual history to come would be to explain how economics, which had "eschewed most considerations of the specificity of markets" subsequently managed to convince others that it "possessed special expertise to construct all manner of actual usable markets, tailor-made for their narrowly specified purposes" (2007, 218). This is partly what his project with Nik-Khah is about, taking up the history of the relation between information theory and economics provided in *Machine Dreams* (Mirowski 2002) by writing the history of the economics of information and extending it up to the present.[5] This history is one where the market becomes an information processor, tasked with the epistemic challenge of "serving as the primary mechanism for the validation of truth" (Mirowski in Lash and Dragos 2016, 130), as Foucault had already recognized. What Nik-Khah and Mirowski add to Foucault's account is the role information theory plays in this story, and that this is closely related to the influence of Hayek, so that "you can't understand the spread of the idea of a market as an information processor without understanding the concomitant rise of neoliberalism" (130).

Contrary to prevalent historical accounts of Hayek's work, Nik-Khah and Mirowski argue that there are three phases to Hayek's view on information, which lead to different schools of market design. The first phase is part of the Socialist Calculation Controversy, where Hayek argues that knowledge is dispersed and therefore planning faces huge epistemological difficulties, but the market can act as a "mechanism for the communication of information." This view is today visible in what our authors (in their 2017 book) call the Walrasian School of Design, but do not discuss further here. A media theory might want to intervene here to revisit the earlier controversies, since some important recent work by Eden Medina on Project Cybersyn in Chile (2014) and by Ben Peters on the Soviet Internet (2016) offers not just a conceptual but technological history of socialist calculation. Even if these are mostly histories of failure or at least of premature endings, they certainly demonstrate that for many the controversy was not simply won by Hayek, and perhaps these histories of media provide different avenues for thinking (and designing) alternatives to neoliberal markets.

The second phase of Hayek's views on information and knowledge, where knowledge is considered to be not just inarticulate but tacit and inaccessible, and the market's role is to make this knowledge accessible for calculation, corresponds to the Bayes-Nash School of Design. Here Hayek considers rationality itself to be largely unconscious. It would be curious for media theorists to read this Hayek alongside the recent work of N. Katherine Hayles on the cognitive nonconscious (2017), perhaps to note some correspondences and differences between neoliberal economics and theories of the nonhuman. Importantly, where Hayek's view on unconscious rationality leads to an evacuation of knowledge from the human, so that the human is mired in radical ignorance while the market provides ultimate truth, Hayles does provide an account of human-machine assemblages in which the human is not simply stupid or ignorant.

Hayek's third view further displaces the human as the subject of knowledge, where he introduces a "species of *knowledge not 'known' by any individual human being at all*" (Nik-Khah and Mirowski, this volume, emphasis in original), with Hayek then replacing the term *knowledge* with the term *information.* Where the individual actor becomes ignorant, the market in turn becomes a "Super Information Processor." This in Nik-Khah and Mirowski's account leads to the Experimentalist School of Design, which, acknowledging its debt to Hayek, focuses on computational capacities of markets, doesn't trust agents and their cognitive capacities, and offloads the task of information processing onto markets in designing "smart markets."

Our authors contend that this is the school of market design that is winning out, and in their discussion of Alvin Roth's work in the concluding section of their chapter, they show what bleak futures this envisions and prepares for us. Economists have become apolitical pragmatists, who design markets for every part of our lives, with the help of artificial intelligence. These markets operate no longer for what people want, but regardless of their wants. We offload thinking onto markets, which are increasingly designed to be devoid of people; only engineering economists have a stake and agency in their operation.[6]

Cathedrals of Computation and Finance

Now at this point one might take a step back and return to Jameson's gesture. Here we find a not so-illicit and more-than-metaphorical association of markets with media—no longer with television but with computers. More precisely, as market design embraces computation and artificial intelligence, it enters what Ian Bogost (2015) has called the "cathedral of computation," where computers are imbued with theological powers, which rub off on markets. Yet the association between markets and media is now even more direct: markets are designed on the basis of digital media technologies. This is perhaps most visible in automated trading in financial markets, and particularly in high-frequency trading. These developments build on a long history in which financial markets "have been structured by the close connection between price formation on stock exchanges and innovations in media technology," as Vogl (2015, 75) recounts with reference to the telegraph, the ticker tape, and other media of markets. These media technologies seem archaic in light of the "billion-dollar technological arms race" that has gripped the global financial market as "the world's largest and most powerful techno-social system" (Johnson et al. 2013, 1).[7]

We can witness this, for example, when providers of market infrastructure drill through mountains to provide more direct links between exchanges, for the purpose of shaving a few milliseconds off information flows in which the speed of light comes to matter as a natural limit to the speed of trading (MacKenzie et al. 2012). In high-frequency trading, every millisecond counts. The introduction of microwaves and other technologies to overcome latency has created further information inequalities at different speeds; the focus on information equality in co-location facilities at data centers demonstrates rather than alleviates this (Zook and Grote 2017). In this way, high-frequency trading perpetuates concentrations of wealth and power (Golumbia 2013). Yet these may also be undermined, as these media technologies achieve what the neoliberals imagined. As Michael Lewis famously explored in *Flash Boys,* the same market does not exist for everyone—you may never be able to buy or sell at a price given to you, if a high-frequency trader has faster access to the order book of the exchange and can front-run you (see Lanchester 2014). The result of this, ultimately, is that no agent can know the market, since no one can rely on the data provided—only "the market" knows.

The social studies of markets and finance literature is perhaps the closest we have already to a media studies of markets. Some of this literature explicitly builds upon Mirowski's earlier work on information in markets and introduces a consideration of media. Consider, for example, Juan Pablo Pardo-Guerra's (2010) work on the automatization of the London Stock Exchange, which argues that the category of information in markets is not given but is constructed in sociotechnical assemblages of financial markets, which change with media revolutions. Pardo-Guerra "socializes" the category of information in this way via a media history of markets. Or consider recent work by Tero Karppi and Kate Crawford (2016) exploring, through the example of the "hack crash" of April 23, 2013, caused by a hacked AP Twitter account announcing a terrorist attack on the White House, the infrastructural relations of social media and automated financial trading. In their view, these algorithmic connections produce a kind of machine ecology among other things displacing the human as a knowledgeable market actor. Ann-Christina Lange, Marc Lenglet, and Robert Seyfert also note, in their introduction to a collection on cultures of high-frequency trading, how the centrality of questions of "epistemic uncertainty" in high-frequency trading results from "the promise . . . that objectivity and profitability can be realized through the use of numerical codes and material infrastructures" (2016, 161).

How would a media theory of markets, informed by Nik-Khah and Mirowski's work on the complicity of market design with neoliberalism, build upon this work? Now, even a cursory reading of those parts of the literature informed by actor-network theory (ANT) specifically shows very quickly that much of it is far removed from the kind of political and critical program that Nik-Khah and Mirowski propose here in their reading of engineering economics and market design as neoliberal. In fact, our authors have elsewhere (Mirowski and Nik-Khah 2008) expressed serious criticisms vis-à-vis particular varieties of this work proposed by Bruno Latour, Michel Callon, and Donald MacKenzie. In brief, their point of criticism is that the presumed "performativity" of economics, which specifically the more recent variants of ANT engages, is far too congruent with the neoliberal project of constructing markets. The authority of neoliberal economists in constructing markets is too easily taken for granted, very little is added to the account of the market designers, and ANT aligns itself politically with their work. In doing so, ANT doesn't acknowledge the specificity of the actors from economics (such as game theorists or experimental economists) and their divergent agendas, and they discount and ignore other key actors in political economy such as states and corporations—but also media.

There are, however, parts of the literature on high-frequency trading that do take the "notorious quasi-material shape-shifter the computer" (Mirowski and Nik-Khah 2008, 118) left out by ANT into account, and thereby come to the conclusion that the performativity thesis "does not suffice to explain the spatial relations that now perform or shape the interaction that plays out between adaptive algorithms" (Lange 2017, 103; on performativity, see also Schröter 2017). It is this literature, drawing on media theory to understand the topology of financial markets and their media technological constitution, that a media theory of markets could build upon.

Jens Schröter's contribution to this volume picks up here, with an attempt to assess the contribution of the work of Michel Callon and Bruno Latour for a media theory of money. Where, perhaps unexpectedly, in the neoclassical economic tradition discussed by Nik-Khah and Mirowski, by and large "the concept of the market was treated as a general symptom for the phenomenon of exchange itself, and hence rendered effectively redundant" (Mirowski and Nik-Khah 2008, 89–90), Schröter sees money similarly ignored in media theory. The same may be true for economics. David Graeber, in his five-thousand-year history of debt, which is also an anthropological history of money, notes that in economics: "Money is unimportant. Economies—'real economies'—are really vast barter systems" (2011, 44–45). Money is considered necessary but coincidental to generalized exchange in markets. As the latest anthropologist to uncover the economists' "myth of barter" (see Maurer 2013), Graeber insists that money did not come into being as people discovered the limits of barter and wanted to trade more freely in markets. Rather, money comes into being with debt, which requires money in order to be quantified: "money and debt appear on the scene at exactly the same time" (Graeber 2011, 21).

Let's provide a little background to Schröter's undertaking. This critique of two representatives of ANT contributes to a wider project that Schröter is involved in with his collaborator Till Heilmann, namely to constitute and develop a "neo-critical media studies," in which a media theory of money plays a key role (Schröter and Heilmann 2016). Drawing on a resurgence in a critique of political economy after the 2007–8 financial crisis, Schröter and Heilmann seek to reinvigorate a critical media studies that, at least in its German variant (see Horn 2008; Pias 2016), has very little to say about capitalism. They, for example, note that Friedrich Kittler's materialism is not historical or concerned with social or social-technical relations but merely with technical apparatuses, so that it constitutes a materialism not of relations but of things. They liken Kittler's dismissal of the social *tout court* to neoliberal rhetoric ("there is no society" Margaret Thatcher famously proclaimed) and suggest it already points to ANT's equally assertive dismissal of the social. The critical thrust of Kittler's media materialism in that way targets not the economic relations of the capitalist social order, but his historical genealogies unmask only the particular economic interests and strategies of individual actors (Schröter and Heilmann 2016, 10–12).

Schröter and Heilmann suggest that a neo-critical media studies should concentrate on three inputs to establishing a relation between a theory of capitalism and a theory of media: (1) it should systematically explicate the media-theoretical contribution to the description of money, as opposed to economic, philosophical, and sociological conceptualizations; (2) it should historically develop a "monetary media archaeology" that understands media history to be essentially marked by the forms and functions of money; and (3) this should lead not only to a historical reformulation but also a critical evaluation of media history, in which technics, as a specific form in which capitalist sociality reproduces itself, appears in its historicity and contingency (2016, 22–23). Money, then, is the potential link between a theory of media and a theory of capital; it becomes central to making media studies critical and to a media theoretical contribution to the critique of capital. Money offers itself up as *the* capitalist medium, as a medium that makes capital possible and potentially makes all other media capitalist. Schröter's contribution here, then, is part, alongside some other preliminary texts (Schröter 2011; 2016), of a project to sketch this media theory of money, which will also yield a book. Yet apart from an empirical observation that media seem to determine our situation, and the preliminary discussions of money as a medium in Marshall McLuhan and elsewhere, why is money so central for Schröter?

Key to Schröter's understanding of money is his engagement with contemporary Marxian theoretical currents. Where on previous occasions Schröter already called for an encounter of media studies with Marx and diverse Marxist traditions (see Schröter et al. 2006),[8] here and elsewhere (in particular Schröter 2011) he builds on the tradition of the "critique of value," which is only slowly being received in Anglophone debates (see Larsen et al. 2014 for a collection of translated texts in the journal *Mediations*). This current, which is organized around the two German-language online journals *Krisis* and *Exit!,* is perhaps most well-known for its critique of Marxist and social democratic politics embracing labor. It sees labor as a coercive social principal, with labor subsumed in the machinations of capital as its other, so that labor is something not to be freed but something we need to free ourselves from—the "Manifesto Against Labour" ends with the demand: "Workers of all countries, call it a day!" (Krisis-Group 1999). This Marxian current thus distinguishes itself quite significantly from other currents such as cultural Marxism or autonomist Marxism, also with regards to its emphasis on circulation and the dominance of the valorization of value as the primary force of history in capitalism, as its "automatic subject" (Kurz 1999; Schröter 2011), leading to a structural crisis of capitalism.

Money is central here, since, as Robert Kurz puts it: "Within this system, money is the tangible form of the appearance of value, which is linked to itself. In the self-expanding movement of capital, which breeds money out of money, money becomes a relentless and restless end-in-itself" (1999, np). The valorization of value—the very definition of capital—is an end-in-itself, as the authors regularly state, and money is its medium. Schröter (2011, 222–23) explicates how in the critique of value money appears as "*Selbstzweck-Medium,*" as "medium as end-in-itself," that is, as the medium that represents the most abstract form value can take in its self-valorization. We can see how, if Schröter follows this line of analysis, money can be understood as the most important and widespread medium today that determines our situation.[9] It is also *the* medium of capital, and dealing with money may also lead us to a critique of capital. Yet is the concept of money as medium we find in the critique of value already sufficient, so that there would be no task left for media theory except to adapt it? For Schröter this is clearly not the case. Kurz certainly provides a clue and challenge for a media theory of money when he writes: "abstract wealth in the form of money is by its nature limitless and interminable, and only its material content is subject to an absolute historical limit"; and "there can be no accumulation without its material bearer, however much the latter's absence would be the ideal of capital" (Kurz in Larsen et al. 2014, 50).

Yet it is not clear at all whether Kurz here and elsewhere also considers money as a "material bearer" of value. But it must certainly bug a media theorist that precisely these Marxians, who insist regularly on the necessity precisely to not ignore materiality, when it comes to money seem to systematically ignore or at least neglect its materiality and mediality, because they see in it the most abstract and pure—and therefore immaterial—form of capital. At the same time, conversely, it clearly bothers Schröter that media theory pays so little attention to the abstractions of capital. For example, in a critique of general ecology—a competing contemporary current of media theory associated with Erich Hörl (see Hörl 2015, and most recently Hörl 2017)—Schröter (2014) laments how there the future of media is discussed without reference to the social or economic relations that mark them, and he sets out to uncover the "economic unconscious" of general ecology. If we set this project alongside Kurz's consideration of how capitalist abstraction marks reality, where he notes that it "is through money that society encounters its own unconscious abstraction as an independent, alienated power" (1999), we can see how money becomes the primary means by which to uncover the economic unconscious of media theory, and of our times.

Elements of a Media Theory of Money

Schröter, then, explores media theory to develop an understanding of the mediality and materiality of money. Before proceeding with his critique of Callon and Latour, he gathers elements of a media theory of money from existing, mostly German media theory. He argues against those, such as Norbert Bolz and Jochen Hörisch, who, in drawing on Niklas Luhmann's definition of money as "symbolically generalized medium of exchange," see money as mostly an abstract, immaterial medium. Considering the relation between the symbolism and materialism of money, Schröter notes that certainly the materiality and mediality of money is not simply an "earthly remainder" which capital will one day be able to abandon (see the discussion of Kurz above). Rather, agreeing with Walter Seitter and Hartmut Winkler, money always relies on material infrastructures and law, so that its materiality, Schröter argues, constitutes "*a very precondition of the operability of money as such*" (this volume, emphasis in original). Trust in money is precisely a question of the relation between the symbolic and infrastructural in money. This is for Schröter the "first, decisive step toward an analysis of money from the perspective of media theory."

To proceed, Schröter suggests engaging with other disciplines such as philosophy, sociology, and economics in search of traces of a media theory of money. We would add anthropology, which perhaps offers the most detailed history of money, with some implicit media archaeology (see Maurer 2006). This literature also becomes key in considering Schröter's argument that follows. He suggests there are two key aspects that qualify materials as potential money: durability and countability. Money must be durable so that it can act as store of value and can travel the distances of trade. It must be countable so that it can serve as a measure of value, and to attach numbers as values to things. Here Schröter notes, drawing on Seitter and Alexander Galloway, that money is already digital, that this already makes the mathematization of production implicit to capitalism, and that therefore "Capitalism is from its very beginning the formalization and digitization of economy, even of society as a whole." While this in itself challenges contemporary accounts of the digital economy, the central argument Schröter makes follows. Because money can be counted, practices of counting proliferate, and there can be more or less of everything.

Schröter concludes (emphasis in original): *"The countable, digital specificity of money leads (at least potentially) to the phenomenon of accumulation."*

Let's pause for a moment to consider the implications of this statement. A weak interpretation would be that capital requires money, that there can be no capital without money, since nothing can be accumulated and thereby no valorization of value can take place. There would be little reason to contest this historically or conceptually. Yet Schröter also seems to imply more: it is because of money that capital can exist and comes into being in the first place. While accumulation is impossible without money, money itself leads—"at least potentially"—to accumulation. That is certainly an unusual assertion, considering various accounts of the emergence of capitalism, in which money does not play such a central role—notwithstanding the economists' "myth of barter" in which money is invented to make generalized commodity exchange (another definition of capitalism) possible. Now, Schröter hesitates to expand on these strong implications of his statement, turning it into a question of the relation between the medium of money and society, in which he wants to avoid a certain media determinism. He suggests that "this complicated problem (which at least is the problem of the emergence of capitalism as such) is better described as a kind of *co-constitution* of money and capital" (this volume, emphasis in original).

What could this co-constitution amount to? A cursory glance at anthropological literature on money questions this coincidence of money and capital *tout court.* By now quite notoriously, Graeber (2011) writes the history of money as the history of debt, and, as we noted above, money enters the stage of history with debt—not with capital. We encounter various kinds of money before we encounter capital, both in Graeber's story and also in other anthropological histories and contemporary accounts of money (see Maurer 2006; 2015). In fact, Graeber notes that certain kinds of interest-bearing loans, as early forms of debt, even "appear to predate writing" (Graeber 2011, 64)—which can only lead to speculation as to how such loans were accounted for. How then can we insist, with Schröter, that money coincides with capital? Do Graeber and the anthropologists perhaps have a different conception of money, or does the money they encounter follow different, noncapitalist scripts? One aspect of Graeber's account is potentially congruent with Schröter's argument. Graeber notes that a consequence of the imposition by states and the subsequent extensive use of money led to a different relation to objects and value. At the origins of capitalism, we don't find "the gradual destruction of traditional communities by the impersonal power of the market"; instead, we discover how "an economy of credit was converted into an economy of interest" (Graeber 2011, 332).

Money in Graeber's account destroys relations of credit that formed social life before it was separated into realms of the economy and all else, and the economy of interest is marked by a morality that demands that interest be paid on debt, in that sense foreshadowing the valorization of value. Graeber's insight potentially refines Schröter's argument, which could in this way take into account how state currencies precipitated the birth of capitalism, and how money was perhaps imbued with the kinds of scripts that make it coincide with capital. This is also key in relation to current discussions around the design of alternative currencies such as Bitcoin (see Lovink et al. 2015). Schröter notes how Micronesian stone money might have been imbued with an excessive materiality precisely to block accumulation. Bitcoin, the most notorious of the new cryptocurrencies, today tries something similar, in that bitcoins are limited and at one point mining bitcoins for the verification of the blockchain will no longer be possible. Now Bitcoin can hardly be offered here as a currency that eschews capital; as David Golumbia (2016) has forcefully argued, Bitcoin expresses a certain "right-wing extremism" in that its open avoidance of state regulation and taxation and its media technological setup mean it has become an object of speculation and extremely unequal distribution of wealth. Nonetheless, Bitcoin does not simply seem to provide the same kinds of scripts as state currencies, and for a media theory of money it may well be worthwhile to explore how these scripts work and where they lead us.

Schröter also mentions financial derivatives in passing, noting that they stem from the same "basic mathematical logic of money" we mentioned above. That may be the case, yet what kind of discontinuities with earlier forms of money mark derivatives? Accounts like those of Dick Bryan and Michael Rafferty in their book on capitalism with derivatives (2006) suggest that much is at stake. They acknowledge that derivatives "perform functions integral to accumulation" (2006, 5) and that, "as a commodification of risk, derivatives are a form of calculation and market transaction that is intrinsic to the logic of a capitalist economy" (8). Yet they also note that derivatives "are bringing some profound changes to the way capitalism is organized: changes as fundamental as the nature of capitalist ownership, the nature of money, and the process of competition" (9). Derivatives have become a kind of "*meta-capital* whose distinctive role is to bind and blend different sorts of 'particular' capital together," providing monetary functions in allowing different bits of capital to be priced (13), and thereby intensifying competition between capital and putting pressure on labor. More than simply continuing previous scripts, then, derivatives and their (post–Black-Scholes) scripts confirm and extend Schröter's account of the coincidence of money and capital: money's scripts are dependent upon its mediality, and with derivatives money's coincidence with capital takes on new qualities.

Repressions of ANT

At this point we can briefly discuss Schröter's critique of Michel Callon and Bruno Latour. Schröter turns to ANT for a conceptualization of the determinations of money, but what he finds is a repression of money and the disregard in Callon and Latour of some basic postulates of ANT, which he seeks to recover for a media theory of money. There are two points to Schröter's criticism of Callon's understanding of capitalism. First, as Callon denies that Capitalism with a capital "C" exists, Schröter accuses him of a "praxeological fallacy": for Callon there are lots of capitalisms with a small "c," but how can we even call these capitalisms when we don't acknowledge that there is something like "capital" that they have in common? For Schröter, this makes little sense and a "radical praxeocentrism" is "*logically impossible*" (emphasis in original). Second, although Schröter acknowledges that Callon's work on calculative devices is quite useful for understanding how markets are constituted, what is missing in Callon for Schröter is any account of value. It is simply unclear what is calculated, and "value" largely only appears in Callon's text as a moral term, not an economic one.

Now for Callon the point of focusing on practices of calculation is precisely to negate the idea that there is a "great divide" between capitalism and its prehistory. Here Schröter returns to money. Whereas he agrees with Callon that money and therefore calculation exists prior to capitalism, what matters is that with the rise of capitalism, society comes to be centered around money and its scripts: namely M-C-M'—that is, the valorization of value in which money is transformed into commodities and back again in order to yield more money. Although devices are supposed to play a central role in Callon's approach, Schröter argues that Callon "follows the neoclassical mainstream's exclusion and oblivion of money," and thereby ignores money as a medium with certain scripts. Where he also follows the economists is in focusing on markets rather than production. For Callon commodities are framed as such; only the framing of things in markets with the help of money turns them into commodities. Schröter argues that this is simply false, since a capitalist society is precisely one in which commodities are produced for markets. In proceeding in this way, Callon erases the basic logic of capitalism, by tearing apart the relation of money and the commodity in the process of accumulation.

This becomes particularly apparent to Schröter in a discussion of a quote by Callon in which he discusses how money's symbolism can easily be changed, e.g. when a grandmother gives her grandchild a silver coin, which the grandchild subsequently doesn't treat as money. Schröter considers this to be beside the point—money is money, and even if the grandmother were to create "private money," the latter can't be considered money at all. Money has "*an irreducible script that cannot be easily changed by different practices*" (emphasis in original), but Callon simply ignores this script. Now the anthropological accounts, including the one by Viviana Zelizer on which Callon draws (see also Maurer 2006; Graeber 2011), partially support Schröter's critique of Callon in that they wouldn't suggest that money's scripts can so easily be changed. Yet these accounts also point to how, in history, there have often been many moneys in existence, and they have produced their own economies. As contemporary work for example with regards to mobile money like M-Pesa (Maurer 2015) shows, mobile money functions to a certain extent independently of state currencies. Certainly, most of the examples of mobile money are pegged to state currencies, but they also in certain ways defy commensurability, and the control of their volume exceeds the capacities of central banks. Schröter rightly points out that M-Pesa and other kinds of mobile money aren't "private money" but stand in a complex relation to state currencies. The challenge here is, then, to explain how money's scripts remain stable despite the ways the symbolism of money is adapted in practice, and how state currencies relate to other moneys and remain dominant despite other moneys that offer potentially different forms of exchange and equivalence.

Schröter's critique of Latour proceeds along similar lines. Schröter doesn't deny that it might be productive to think of money as an immutable mobile, but there are two ways in which Latour treats money that disturb him. The first is that Latour seems to insist on the symmetry of immutable mobiles, whereas for Schröter this would be a premise but not a conclusion one can arrive at once we notice how money determines our situation. Money also determines other immutable mobiles due to its centrality in capitalist societies; it is therefore "precisely not *one immutable mobile among others,* but their *conditio sine qua non*" (emphasis in original). In a footnote Schröter qualifies this and notes that one better speaks of "a kind of interdependent accretion" of different media, in which however "money is ultimately, unlike other immutable mobiles, never dispensable." The second criticism of Latour is that his whole model is based on assuming there is an agonistic situation, and that immutable mobiles are enrolled to assert one's position. For Schröter, this assumption is unacceptable for an ANT that seeks to avoid universals and doesn't prefer any kinds of social aggregates. Yet much like Thomas Hobbes's "war of all against all," Latour seems to presume that we are always already stuck in a competitive, agonistic situation. Latour seems to precisely assume the market to be ahistorical, whereas its institution needs to be explained. Money seems to be the model for immutable mobiles, but, Schröter argues, this is repressed.

Schröter doesn't stop with a total dismissal of Callon, Latour, and ANT. Rather, he wants to rescue ANT from the "*double repression of money in the discourse of ANT*: One concerning the relation between money and human actors and one concerning the relation between money and nonhuman actors" (emphasis in original). What would an actor-network theory look like without this double repression? Perhaps some of this is already visible in the kinds of social studies of finance and markets we explored above. Recent work in economic anthropology, drawing quite extensively on traditions of ANT, might also yield some important contributions on which a media theory of money could build, by focusing on capitalization as a notion "indefectibly related, more or less literally, to the mundane idea of *capital*: money, or something comparable, that can be used to make more money, or something comparable" (Collectif CSI 2017, 12).

At the very end of his contribution, Schröter suggests that the critique of money might point to "the possibilities of postmonetary societal structures." If, in doing so, we want to avoid Proudhonist traps and the fantasy that by simply getting rid of money we can also get rid of capital, Kurz warns that the "emancipatory 'abolition of money' is only possible in the context of an abolition of the labor-substance, its value-form, and the complementary, socially extrinsic state machine" (1999, np). Schröter would presumably concur, which means that, as long as we are not content with building alternative currencies that might lead to some (minor?) alternatives within capitalism, a media theory might also need to think about contributing to a more extensive project of critiquing and dismantling capital. At least that seems to be in the cards for Schröter.

||||||||||||||||

This volume, then, searches for media in markets through various pathways. Edward Nik-Khah and Philip Mirowski primarily concentrate on unmasking contemporary economists occupied with market design as neoliberals in their adherence to key precepts of Hayekian information theory. Since information theory is key to understanding contemporary economics, and economists are involved in building markets also with the help of media technologies, media studies here face the challenge of coming to terms with how dominant the computer has become as a metaphor, model, and actual media technological basis of markets. Rather than becoming handmaidens of the neoliberal market designers (Mirowski and Nik-Khah 2008), media theory is here invited to consider how it can contribute both to unmasking how the dominance of markets is supported by the metaphorical power of computers in the "cathedrals of computation" (Bogost 2015), and to conceiving alternatives to the dominance of neoliberal markets, perhaps in drawing on contemporary work in media studies that conceives of other forms of computing the economy and different human–machine relations (Medina 2014; Peters 2016; Hayles 2017), as well as work in the social studies of finance and markets.

Jens Schröter focuses on excavating a media theory of money from existing media theory and drawing on the Marxian tradition of the critique of value. Money determines our situation, in Schröter's view, and in exploring how precisely money as the primary medium of capital's valorization of value conditions both other media and the world around us in general, media theory can contribute to a burgeoning critique of capital. To do so, however, it must first excise its own economic unconscious. The challenge for media studies here will be to establish its contribution to a theory of money and a critique of capital, and perhaps to consider its role in designing different forms of money, whether cryptocurrencies or mobile moneys, which may not be so easily amenable to capitalist accumulation, and which would certainly have to escape Silicon Valley's not-so-unconscious economic drives in the form of venture capital and speculation on our media technological futures. Recent debates around commons propose an end to capitalism, with the commons as the cell-form of a "commonism" opposed to the commodity as the cell-form of capital (see Beverungen et al. 2013). While these commons might require their special kind of money that defies accumulation (see Terranova and Fumagalli in Lovink et al. 2015), efforts are also underway to conceive of societies beyond money.[10] This invention of life beyond money is certainly a task beyond media theory (see also Berardi in Lovink et al. 2015).

Now, this is a volume in search of media in markets, and perhaps it is symptomatic of media studies' economic unconscious that the term that was set here isn't "capital," even if, more or less explicitly, both contributions are framed in larger projects involving precisely a critique of neoliberal capital. Yet, this roundabout way, proceeding via markets and money, might still be a suitable path. Michael Mayer (2006) has taken the direct path in considering capital as medium. He importantly refers to colonial history, specifically to Christopher Columbus's "discovery" of the New World as thoroughly determined by capitalist speculation and the preparation of that new world for capital accumulation, and to Adam Smith's blindness toward slavery as an effect of capital understood as an operational medium or dispositif that does not see what it systematically denies (i.e. the colonial and other violence of primitive accumulation). Mayer sees, extending Foucault, the "totally economized life" as having become a fact since 1989 (Mayer 2016, 129), and he tries to account for it via capital as a medium that shapes our relationship to reality and can be read in its performative effect. Yet this life precisely becomes decipherable not through reference to an "autonomous market" or its "invisible hand" (even if these are understood as features of a programmatic marketization) but through the combined projects that Nik-Khah and Mirowski and Schröter propose here: a sociohistorical account of the politico-scientific neoliberal project, and a media-archaeological account of money as medium of capital.

Mayer's conclusion that "capital as medium determines our situation" (2016, 145) certainly chimes with Schröter's contribution, but it is precisely a move away from a focus on capital as an abstract worldview or relation, which still reverberates in Mayer's text, toward a focus on markets, money, and their media technologies that offers much more explanatory power for the history of capital and its medial constitutions. In taking on such a task, this contribution suggests, media studies must also take stock of some of the key traditions that have shaped the field, whether these derive from Marxism, Foucault, Kittler, or ANT, and to engage with key debates today, for example around financial markets, cryptocurrencies, and mobile money, in which we can already perceive a media theory to come. In that way, media studies might be able to escape the capitalist realism (Fischer 2009) that marks future visions of cybernetic capitalism (*Tiqqun* 2001) and that is enabled and sustained also by media technologies.

Notes

1. "Neoliberalism" is a widely used yet highly contested term, and media theorists might be hesitant to use it. For reasons why it is an indispensable term for political-economic analysis today, see Mirowski (2014) and Davies (2016).
2. What is noteworthy about Fukuyama (1992) is that he speaks of liberalism and free-market economics rather than neoliberalism. For a comment on how financial markets imagine an end of history where the future "is always already priced in," see Vogl (2015, 80–82).
3. As the website cheerfully pronounces: "Combining the philosophies behind two of Thomas Edison's greatest inventions—the ticker-tape and the Victrola: TickTrola converts stock data to tones so that you can keep your ear on the market!" See http://www.geneffects.com/ticktrola/.
4. A brief history of the media of financial markets is available in Reichert (2009, 83–157).
5. See Lash and Dragos (2016) for a useful interview in which Mirowski outlines

what is at stake in his current project and how it relates to his intellectual work so far. See Golumbia (2017) for a preliminary account of Mirowski as a critic of the digital.

6 Here, apart from the history of information theory and neoliberalism, one might also wonder how this constitutes another chapter in the forms of non-knowledge that digital cultures bring forth. See Bernard et al. (2018).

7 Schröter suggests elsewhere (Schröter and Heilmann 2016, 20) that this speed-up of trade is caused not by computers but is programmed by the escalation of the logic of accumulation of capital. We will discuss this below with reference to derivatives.

8 This edited collection of texts on media and Marx already includes a chapter on the medium money (Gernalzick 2006). Curiously, Schröter does not reference this text, presumably because it rather restrictively (with the help of Schumpeter) characterizes Marx as a metallist, considers Marx's theory of value to be outdated and in need of abandonment, and summarily dismisses the work of Robert Kurz, a key representative of the "critique of value" stream of Marxian thought, as unscientific. As we will see shortly, both the theory of value and the work of Kurz are central to Schröter's arguments here.

9 Bill Maurer, in his book on technology and the future of money, notes that the mobile phone is "the second-most ubiquitous technology after money" (2015, 34), which explains why mobile money has become a terrain of experimentation, as we will discuss below.

10 "Society after Money" is precisely the title of a research project in which Jens Schröter is involved alongside sociologists, economists, and commons-theorists, among others. See http://nach-dem-geld.de/projekt/.

References

Bernard, Andreas, Matthias Koch, and Martina Leeker, eds. 2018. *Non-Knowledge and Digital Cultures.* Lüneburg: meson press.

Beverungen, Armin, Anna-Maria Murtola, and Gregory Schwartz. 2013. "The Communism of Capital?" *ephemera* 13, no. 3: 483–95.

Bogost, Ian. 2015. "The Cathedral of Computation." *The Atlantic,* January 15. Accessed May 20, 2017. https://www.theatlantic.com/technology/archive/2015/01/the-cathedral-of-computation/384300/.

Brown, Wendy. 2015. *Undoing the Demos: Neoliberalism's Stealth Revolution.* New York: Zone Books.

Bryan, Dick, and Michael Rafferty. 2006. *Capitalism with Derivatives: A Political Economy of Financial Derivatives, Capital, and Class.* New York: Palgrave Macmillan.

Collectif CSI. 2017. *Capitalization: A Cultural Guide.* Paris: Presses des Mines.

Davies, Will. 2016. "The Difficulty of 'Neoliberalism.'" *Political Economy Research Centre,* January 1. Accessed May 20, 2017. http://www.perc.org.uk/project_posts/the-difficulty-of-neoliberalism/.

Fisher, Mark. 2009. *Capitalist Realism: Is There No Alternative?* Winchester: Zero Books.

Foucault, Michel. 2008. *The Birth of Biopolitics: Lectures at the Collège de France, 1978–79,* ed Michel Senellart and trans. Graham Burchell. New York: Palgrave Macmillan.

Fukuyama, Francis. 1992. *The End of History and the Last Man.* New York: Free Press.

Geoghegan, Bernard Dionysius. 2016. "The Spirit of Media: An Introduction." *Critical Inquiry* 42, no. 4: 809–14.

Gernalzick, Nadja. 2006. "Medium Geld." In *Media Marx: Ein Handbuch,* ed. Jens Schröter, Gregor Schwering, and Urs Stäheli, 85–103. Masse Und Medium 4. Bielefeld: transcript.

Golumbia, David. 2013. "High-Frequency Trading: Networks of Wealth and the Concentration of Power." *Social Semiotics* 23, no. 2: 278–99.

Golumbia, David. 2016. *The Politics of Bitcoin: Software as Right-Wing Extremism.* Minneapolis: University of Minnesota Press.

Golumbia, David. 2017. "Mirowski as a Critic of the Digital." Presentation at *boundary 2* Symposium *Neoliberalism, Its Ontology and Genealogy: The Work and Context of Philip Mirowksi.* University of Pittsburgh, March 16–17.

Graeber, David. 2011. *Debt: The First 5,000 Years.* Brooklyn, N.Y.: Melville House.

Hayles, Katherine. 2017. *Unthought: The Power of the Cognitive Nonconscious*. Chicago: The University of Chicago Press.

Heidenreich, Ralph, and Stefan Heidenreich. 2008. *Mehr Geld.* Berlin: Merve Verlag.

Hörl, Erich, ed. 2017. *General Ecology: The New Ecological Paradigm.* London: Bloomsbury.

Hörl, Erich. 2015. "The Technological Condition," trans. Anthony Enns. *Parrhesia* 22, no. 1: 1–15.

Horn, Eva. 2008. "Editor's Introduction: 'There Are No Media.'" *Grey Room* 29:6–13.

Jameson, Fredric. 1991. *Postmodernism, or The Cultural Logic of Late Capitalism*. Durham, N.C.: Duke University Press.

Johnson, Neil, Guannan Zhao, Eric Hunsader, Hong Qi, Nicholas Johnson, Jing Meng, and Brian Tivnan. 2013. "Abrupt Rise of New Machine Ecology beyond Human Response Time." *Scientific Reports* 3 (September). Accessed May 20, 2017. https://www.nature.com/articles/srep02627.

Jones, Campbell. 2013. *Can the Market Speak?* Winchester: Zero Books.

Karppi, Tero, and Kate Crawford. 2016. "Social Media, Financial Algorithms, and the Hack Crash." *Theory, Culture & Society* 33, no. 1: 73–92.

Krisis-Group. 1999. "Manifesto against Labour." *Krisis,* December 31. Accessed May 20, 2017. http://www.krisis.org/1999/manifesto-against-labour/.

Kurz, Robert. 1999. "Marx 2000." Exit Online. https://www.exit-online.org/link.php?tab=transnationales&kat=English&ktext=Marx%202000.

Lanchester, John. 2014. "Scalpers Inc." *London Review of Books,* June 5. https://www.lrb.co.uk/v36/n11/john-lanchester/scalpers-inc.

Lange, Ann-Christina, Marc Lenglet, and Robert Seyfert. 2016. "Cultures of High-Frequency Trading: Mapping the Landscape of Algorithmic Developments in Contemporary Financial Markets." *Economy and Society* 45, no. 2: 149–65.

Lange, Ann-Christina. 2017. "The Noisy Motions of Instruments: The Performative Space of High-Frequency Trading." In *Performing the Digital: Performativity and*

Performance Studies in Digital Cultures, ed. Martina Leeker, Imanuel Schipper, and Timon Beyes, 101–14. Bielefeld: transcript Verlag.

Larsen, Neil, Mathias Nilges, Josh Robinson, and Nicholas Brown, eds. 2014. *Marxism and the Critique of Value,* special issue of *Mediations: Journal of the Marxist Literary Group* 27, no. 1–2. http://www.mediationsjournal.org/toc/27_1.

Lash, Scott, and Bogdan Dragos. 2016. "An Interview with Philip Mirowski." *Theory, Culture & Society* 33, no. 6: 123–40.

Lovink, Geert, Nathaniel Tkacz, and Patricia de Vries. 2015. *Moneylab Reader: An Intervention in Digital Economy*. Amsterdam: Institute of Network Cultures.

MacKenzie, Donald, Daniel Beunza, Yuval Millo, and Juan Pablo Pardo-Guerra. 2012. "Drilling through the Allegheny Mountains: Liquidity, Materiality, and High-Frequency Trading." *Journal of Cultural Economy* 5, no. 3: 279–96.

Maurer, Bill. 2006. "The Anthropology of Money." *Annual Review of Anthropology* 35, no. 1: 15–36.

Maurer, Bill. 2013. "David Graeber's Wunderkammer, *Debt: The First 5 000 Years.*" *Anthropological Forum* 23, no. 1: 79–93.

Maurer, Bill. 2015. *How Would You like to Pay? How Technology Is Changing the Future of Money.* Durham, N.C.: Duke University Press.

Mayer, Michael. 2016. "Kapital als Medium: Zu einer kritischen Theorie des Medialen." *Internationales Jahrbuch Für Medienphilosphie* 2, no. 1: 125–47.

Medina, Eden. 2014. *Cybernetic Revolutionaries: Technology and Politics in Allende's Chile*. Cambridge, Mass.: The MIT Press.

Mirowski, Philip. 2002. *Machine Dreams: Economics Becomes a Cyborg Science.* Cambridge, UK: Cambridge University Press.

Mirowski, Philip. 2007. "Markets Come to Bits: Evolution, Computation, and Markomata in Economic Science." *Journal of Economic Behavior & Organization* 63, no. 2: 209–42.

Mirowski, Philip. 2013. *Never Let a Serious Crisis Go to Waste: How Neoliberalism Survived the Financial Meltdown.* London: Verso.

Mirowski, Philip. 2014. "The Political Movement That Dared Not Speak Its Own Name: The Neoliberal Thought Collective under Erasure." Institute for New Economic Thinking Working Paper 23. Accessed May 20, 2017. https://www.ineteconomics.org/research/research-papers/the-political-movement-that-dared-not-speak-its-own-name-the-neoliberal-thought-collective-under-erasure.

Mirowski, Philip, and Edward Nik-Khah. 2008. "Command Performance: Exploring What STS Thinks It Takes to Build a Market." In *Living in a Material World: Economic Sociology Meets Science and Technology Studies*, ed. Trebor Pinch and Richard Swedberg, 89–128. Cambridge, Mass.: The MIT Press.

Mirowski, Philip, and Edward M. Nik-Khah. 2017. *The Knowledge We Have Lost in Information: The History of Information in Modern Economics.* New York: Oxford University Press.

Pardo-Guerra, Juan Pablo. 2010. "Creating Flows of Interpersonal Bits: The Automation of the London Stock Exchange, c. 1955–90." *Economy and Society* 39, no. 1: 84–109.

Peters, Benjamin. 2016. *How Not to Network a Nation: The Uneasy History of the Soviet Internet.* Cambridge, Mass.: The MIT Press.

Pias, Claus. 2016. "What's German about German Media Theory?" In *Media Transatlantic: Developments in Media and Communication Studies between North American and German-Speaking Europe,* ed. Norm Friesen, 15–27. Cham: Springer International Publishing.

Reichert, Ramon. 2009. *Das Wissen der Börse.* Bielfeld: transcript.

Schröter, Jens. 2011. "Das Automatische Subjekt. Überlegungen Zu Einem Begriff von Karl Marx." In *Unsichtbare Hände: Automatismen in Medien-, Technik- und Diskursgeschichte,* ed. Hannelore Bublitz, Irina Kaldrack, Theo Röhle, and Hartmut Winkler. Munich: Wilhelm Fink.

Schröter, Jens. 2014. "The Future of the Media, General Ecology, and Its Economic Unconscious." *Wi: Journal of Mobile Media* 8, no. 2. Accessed May 20, 2017. http://wi.mobilities.ca/wp-content/uploads/2014/11/schr%C3%B6ter_future_of_media.pdf.

Schröter, Jens. 2017. "Performing the Economy, Digital Media, and Crisis: A Critique of Michel Callon." In *Performing the Digital: Performativity and Performance Studies in Digital Cultures,* ed. Martina Leeker, Imanuel Schipper, and Timon Beyes. Bielefeld: transcript Verlag.

Schröter, Jens, and Till A. Heilmann. 2016. "Zum Bonner Programm einer Neo-Kritischen Medienwissenschaft." *Navigationen: Zeitschrift für Medien- und Kulturwissenschaften* 16, no. 2: 7–36.

Schröter, Jens, Gregor Schwering, and Urs Stäheli, eds. 2006. *Media Marx: Ein Handbuch.* Masse Und Medium 4. Bielefeld: transcript.

Tellmann, Ute. 2009. "Foucault and the Invisible Economy." *Foucault Studies* 6: 5–24.

Tiqqun. 2001. "L'hypothèse Cybernetique." *Tiqqun* 2: 40–83.

Vogl, Joseph. 2015. *The Specter of Capital.* Stanford, Calif.: Stanford University Press.

Zook, Matthew, and Michael H Grote. 2017. "The Microgeographies of Global Finance: High-Frequency Trading and the Construction of Information Inequality." *Environment and Planning A* 49, no. 1: 121–40.

[2]

The Ghosts of Hayek in Orthodox Microeconomics: Markets as Information Processors

Edward Nik-Khah and Philip Mirowski

In media studies, there is recurrent fascination with how communication, especially when couched in terms of "information," tends to influence many spheres of social life and intellectual endeavor. Some of the key figures in that discipline have been especially attentive to the implications for politics of the modern advent of the "information economy." Nevertheless, we think that there has been little impetus among media scholars to explore how other disciplines, and in this case orthodox economics, have been providing competing accounts of the nature and importance of information over the same rough time frame. Furthermore, we think they might be surprised to learn that Friedrich Hayek and the neoliberals have been important in framing inquiry into the information economy for the larger culture for a couple of generations. This essay is a preliminary report on what would happen to intellectual history if media studies took the early development of the "economics of information" into account.

We devote this chapter to asking what "deep impact" Hayek registered on the economics profession. The Austrians, as the caretakers of Hayek's legacy, have tended to subscribe to a unitary Hayek account; the economics orthodoxy has claimed there to be two Hayeks—one good, one bad. Perhaps this is a bit too crude, but we believe that attending more carefully to all the positions Hayek took on agent epistemology and information will lead us to revise the count upward. When we review the history, it becomes apparent that Hayek advanced *three* distinct views. Significantly, each one found its echo in a school of economic thought (the Walrasian School, the Bayes-Nash School, and the Experimentalist School) and informed a corresponding view on the appropriate role for the economist to play in the setup of markets—the most important development within microeconomics over the past two decades. Contrary to both orthodox economists and Austrians, neoliberalism has occupied the profession's heartland, and has planted its flag.

Today, market designers celebrate the market as omnipotent information processor while conflating the pervasive ignorance of market agents with virtue. Against proposals from certain scholars in science and technology studies who promote a "constructivist" approach to markets and seek a potential alliance with market designers (see Mirowski and Nik-Khah 2008), we offer this account of information economics and market design to media studies scholars, in order for them to consider both the dangers of equating the market with the computer as information processor and the more serious epistemological challenges these developments pose for thinking about the role of human–machine relations in society more generally.

Hayek: The Good, the Bad, and the Unitary

Sometimes it is easy to see the beginnings of things and harder to see the ends. During the 1940s, Friedrich Hayek challenged the practicality of central economic planning on informational grounds, providing the impetus for an impressive roster of mathematical neoclassical economists to join in efforts to rebut him. Some may additionally note that it is "interesting" that so many of these figures would go on to play leading roles in the various and sundry research programs that came to be known as "information economics." Even so, the interest has apparently been fleeting: there has been little sober reflection on the full significance of Hayek's role in this episode, and none whatsoever on whether, and in what capacity, he reprised it.

Specifically, most economists would think it absurd to even entertain the thought that Hayek's later work—including not only his scholarship but also the establishment of the Mont Pèlerin Society (MPS), as well as the subsequent development of neoliberalism—was relevant in any way to the historical development of information economics. We know this because a few have felt the need to state for the record that the MPS and the neoliberalism it has espoused has come nowhere near the core of the economics orthodoxy. Of course, the very fact that anyone would feel compelled to defend economics from this charge is an interesting matter in its own right—due in part to the recent appearance of scholarship casting professional economists as important players in the postwar revival of the Right, the outsized representation of MPS members in the roster of Bank of Sweden prizewinners, and the sad cooptation of the profession during the Crisis (see Mirowski and Nik-Khah 2017). Nevertheless, those who have taken it as their business to educate the public on such matters have warranted that there is nothing to see here—perhaps in the macroeconomic hinterlands, but not where the serious science is done.

Take the 1987 Bank of Sweden prizewinner, Robert Solow. Prompted by the publication of one recent history of the postwar rise of "pro-market" thinking, Solow said the following:

> Outside the economics profession, [the MPS] was invisible. The MPS was no more influential inside the economics profession. There were no publications to be

> discussed. The American membership was apparently limited to economists of the Chicago School and its scattered university outposts, plus a few transplanted Europeans. "Some of my best friends" belonged. There was, of course, continuing research and debate among economists on the good and bad properties of competitive and noncompetitive markets, and the capacities and limitations of corrective regulation. But these would have gone on in the same way had the MPS not existed. (Solow 2012)

Of course, it would be absurd to claim that politics were entirely absent from postwar disputes over matters of economic doctrine—but to many, such disputes seem quaint, the holdover of a bygone era and confined to questionable subsets of the profession. Recently, Noah Smith has taken it as his duty and mission to challenge the unprecedented enmity directed at the economics profession suffusing the blogosphere in the wake of the worldwide financial crisis by drawing attention to what he believes to be praiseworthy recent developments; not hiding behind impenetrable mathematics and jargon, Smith assumes the responsibility of taking his argument directly to the public. The title of a recent post of his accurately conveys his central point: "Economists used to be the priests of free markets—now they're just a bunch of engineers" (N. Smith 2014b). According to Smith's understanding of the profession, most economists are prone to focus on small, solvable problems, and uninterested in making sweeping contributions to policy:

> I have the vague sense that if you were an idealistic, brilliant young libertarian in the 1960s and '70s, you might naturally dream of growing up to be an economist. You might watch a rousing speech by Milton Friedman, and you might imagine that one day you, too, would use the power of logic and rationality and mathematics to ward off the insanity of socialism. Well, America still has some idealistic, brilliant young libertarians, and some of them probably still dream of becoming economists. But now they will be in the minority. They will be joined by quite a

> few—maybe more—idealistic brilliant young liberals, who recognize the power of markets but also want to figure out how to fix things when markets go wrong. And they will also be joined by quite a few brilliant engineers, for whom political ideals take a back seat to the solving of practical, real-world problems. Econ isn't what it used to be. (N. Smith 2014b)

He is willing to grant the point, but only for macroeconomists:

> So if you really feel you must get out your rake or pitchfork and storm the gates of the economists who fiddled while our economy burned, go ahead. Just make sure that the people whose heads you are calling for are not in that vast silent majority who are working diligently on the small but solvable problems of "microeconomics." The people at whom you are angry are called "macroeconomists." (N. Smith 2014a)

While one might rightly lament the susceptibility of macroeconomics to ideological capture, the important point for Smith is that microeconomics remains hermetically sealed, protected from anything unsavory.

Economists who acknowledge the significance of Hayek's scholarly contributions while denying that of his assiduous political and organizational efforts face a challenge. Reading the aforementioned Solow provides some indication of how the orthodox economist manages to meet it:

> The Good Hayek was a serious scholar who was particularly interested in the role of knowledge in the economy . . . All economists know that a system of competitive markets is a remarkably efficient way to aggregate all that knowledge while preserving decentralization. (Solow 2012)

The "bad" of Hayek is easily and safely excised: Hayek possessed "intuition" but little else, whereas the modern economist comes equipped with a bracing rigor. Hayek may have posed some interesting questions, but his lack of mathematical sophistication permitted his politics to mar the enterprise. Since then, economists have scrubbed away all its traces. Perhaps true, but Solow provides us no example of how this worked.

For one such example, we may turn to the 2007 Bank of Sweden prizewinner, Eric Maskin:

> Hayek had a remarkable intuitive understanding of some major propositions in mechanism design—and the assumptions they rest on—long before their precise formulation. Indeed, his understanding seems to have been a guiding influence in their formulation. (Maskin 2015, 251)

Maskin's two "Hayekian" propositions are, first, that "competitive markets are informationally efficient" and, second, that "the market mechanism is uniquely incentive compatible." Notwithstanding Hayek's intuition, a firm grasp of formal economic analysis (particularly game theory) eluded him, preventing him from grasping the nettle ("he did not anticipate—as far as I can tell—the Vickrey-Clarke-Groves mechanism for determining a Pareto optimal public goods allocation" (Maskin 2015, 251)). Nevertheless, Maskin describes him as "precursor" (247) and "guiding influence" (251) (as if these would serve as the same thing), even going so far as to make the interesting suggestion that those most involved in developing the game theoretic literature on markets did so with Hayek in mind. Unfortunately, Maskin never seriously pursued this idea any further: probably because he exhibits no more than a bare-bones understanding of the corpus of Hayek's work. Unsurprisingly, both passages Maskin cites in support of his interpretation of Hayek were taken from the same article, "The Use of Knowledge in Society"; neither says anything about "incentive compatibility"; nor does Maskin feel impelled to provide a single specific example of Hayek's guidance.

While the orthodoxy's lack of curiosity concerning its history is in no way surprising, one might have hoped for better when it came to the self-appointed caretakers of Hayek's legacy, the Austrians. But to date, their efforts to address Hayek's influence on the orthodoxy have proved no more insightful. This was nowhere more apparent than in the aftermath of the award of the 2007 Bank of Sweden Prize to Leonid Hurwicz, Maskin, and Roger Myerson. Hurwicz was a chief Walrasian market socialist; his award celebrated his work following a repudiation of his earlier enthusiasms. Initially, some Austrians greeted the occasion with applause, as an acknowledgement of Hayek's worth so incontrovertible as to be undeniable by even the most blinkered orthodox economist.[1] But this position apparently ran up against the perceived need to maintain the distinctiveness of the Austrian approach, not to mention the traditional insistence upon the "articulate" versus "inarticulate" knowledge distinction (which was often used precisely to upbraid Walrasians such as Hurwicz).[2]

So, subsequently, some Austrians executed an about-face and now accused both Walrasians and Bayes-Nash game theorists (such as Maskin and Myerson) alike of "failed appropriation" of Hayek (Boettke and O'Donnell 2013). One might expect that this turnabout would stimulate an interest in pinpointing exactly what it was game theorists sought to appropriate and why.[3] To that end, some Austrians did organize a conference at George Mason, with the laudable intention "to examine and provide us with insights into the impact of Hayek's work on the research direction of other scholars in economics and political economy . . . [to] stimulate a conversation about the deep impact of Hayek's ideas" (Boettke and Coyne 2015).[4] But so far this project was hampered by a commitment to a single monolithic "Hayekian framework," which mainstream approaches to the "economics of information," putatively characterized by a flawed adherence to the "omniscience" of economic agents, could be said to have misunderstood. Unfortunately, the ahistoricity of their approach has induced Austrians to miss the most direct avenues of Hayek's "deep impact" on orthodox economics.

Perceiving this impact will require us to move beyond the 1940s, and to observe how both Hayek and the economics orthodoxy alike grappled with epistemic issues over the subsequent half century.

Hayek Changes His Mind

We begin by recapping a relatively well-known set of events: Austrian neoliberals such as Friedrich Hayek kicked off something known as the "Socialist Calculation Controversy" with an argument that government planners could never know enough to adequately plan any reasonably elaborate economic system. The error of Socialism, said Hayek, was to try and accomplish something through planning that had already been solved by The Market. Hayek suggested that it would be too difficult to collect all the disparate and sundry information to engage in economy-wide planning. We cannot reprise those events here; all we wish to do is highlight that the subsequent disputes tended to get sidetracked into a set of parallel considerations of what it meant for markets to convey "information" to the relevant actors. By the 1940s, the neoliberal argument was largely being promoted by international members of the newly founded Mont Pèlerin Society, while their opponents were primarily located (contrary to modern impressions) at something called the Cowles Commission, located from 1938 to 1952 at the University of Chicago, and thereafter at Yale.

What trace remains of this dispute in the mental maps of the modal economist is found in Hayek's "Use of Knowledge in Society," and aptly summarized by that article's most famous passage:

> What is the problem we try to solve when we try to construct a rational economic order? On certain familiar assumptions the answer is simple enough. *If* we possess all the relevant information, *if* we can start out from a given system of preferences and *if* we command complete knowledge of available means, the problem which remains is purely one of logic . . . This, however, is emphatically *not* the economic problem which society faces . . . The peculiar character of the problem of a rational economic order is determined precisely by the fact that the knowledge of the circumstances of which we must make use never exists in concentrated or integrated form but

> solely as the dispersed bits of incomplete and frequently contradictory knowledge which all the separate individuals possess. The economic problem of society is thus not merely a problem how to allocate "given" resources . . . it is a problem of the utilization of knowledge which is not given to anyone in its totality. (Hayek 1945, 519-20)

The typical attitude toward this passage is exemplified by Maskin (quoted above): it is right and proper that the Bank of Sweden honored him. But 1945 was a long time ago, and the memory of socialism recedes further with every day. Goodbye to all that.

Only recently, with the explosion of historical literature on Hayek, have we begun to encounter serious scholarly work on Hayek's struggles with epistemology.[5] As with almost every other major intellectual figure, Hayek changed his position on key theoretical terms over the course of his career; and none was more consequential than his treatment of knowledge. Interestingly, in Hayek's last book, *The Fatal Conceit,* he admits,

> I confess that it took me too a long time from my first breakthrough, in my essay on "Economics and Knowledge" through the recognition of "Competition as a Discovery Procedure" and my essay on "The Pretense of Knowledge" to state my theory of the dispersal of information, from which follows my conclusions about the superiority of spontaneous formations to central direction. (Hayek 1988, 88)

So while we have his frank admission that his system did not congeal around the concept of *information* until rather late in his career, at least in his own mind, we do not have a corresponding historical schematic of how it changed from his own hand. Leaning on the secondary literature, we will proceed to summarize it as a symphony in three movements.

In the first movement, Hayek displaced the rather cryptic position of Ludwig von Mises in the Socialist Calculation controversy, that all "calculation" whatsoever would be impossible under socialism, and replaced it with the seemingly more credible proposition that it would be impossible to collate and deploy all the knowledge required to coordinate the economy as successfully as the market managed to do in practice. In other words, he transformed what Mises had portrayed as a breakdown of (Max) Weberian zweckrationality under socialism into something initially far less threatening, a species of epistemological difficulty endemic under socialism.[6] For the early Hayek, knowledge was "dispersed" in such a way that bringing it all together in a central planning authority would be difficult—but, note well, *not impossible.* There seemed to be a special kind of slippery knowledge, a sticky goo qualitatively different from more conventional scientific conceptions, that was *local,* characterized by special conditions of time and place.

It was almost as if this species of knowledge was something *entropic*: an energy that grew too diffuse to be readily gathered up and consolidated into a useful form.[7] Not all knowledge shared this character, said Hayek; but the mere fact it existed at all was a club he could use to beat on the Langes and Marschaks of this world. Sometimes Hayek hinted that the dispersed character had something to do with subjective experience, but at this stage he steered well clear of issues of cognitive capacities or capacities to articulate this knowledge to others. In this movement, there was very little in the way of actual epistemology or formal psychology standing behind the concept. Instead, in his famous paper "Use of Knowledge in Society" (1945), he proposes to reconceive the market as a "mechanism for communicating information." Perhaps this is one reason it seemed to appeal to some neoclassical economists, who were more readily inclined to interpret knowledge of this ilk as a "thing" scattered about the landscape, rather like pixie dust too fine to pick up. Indeed, most of the favorable citations of Hayek by neoclassical economists date from this period.

The next movement in Hayek's Surprise Symphony happened sometime around his own return to psychology published in 1952 as *The Sensory Order.* At this stage, Hayek entertained the notion that much of human knowledge is not only inarticulable but also tacit and inaccessible to self-examination. Much of his revised attitudes concerning knowledge seems to have occurred during his stint at the Committee on Social Thought at the University of Chicago. In brief, Hayek there sought to revive the old discredited associationist psychology of the late eighteenth and early nineteenth century, by suggesting mind was little more than sets of hierarchies of systems of classifier algorithms that were opaque to the thinker.[8] He also had been in contact with Michael Polanyi at the early MPS meetings and had come across Gilbert Ryle's distinction between "knowing how" and "knowing that" in Ryle's *Concept of Mind* (1949). He began to explore variations on "tacit" or nonarticulable knowledge, not so much by explicitly following Polanyi or Ryle on this topic as through building his own idiosyncratic theory of mind upon a foundation of classifier systems about which the subject was not even aware of knowing but regularly made use of in order to interact with the environment.[9]

From this point forward, Hayek began to play fast and loose with the concept of consciousness, inverting the then-popular Freudian frame tale that the unconscious was a soup of barely accessible urges upon which rested a fragile vessel of rational thought; for Hayek, it was *rationality that was largely unconscious,* with conscious perception and drives constituting the thin veneer of intentionality and desires floating on top of the sea of obscure and inaccessible rule structures. Thus the types of knowledge that mattered most were inarticulate and largely inaccessible to the thinking agent. It was also precisely at this juncture that Hayek began making explicit references to evolutionary theory as the basis of his entire philosophy. The reason behind this shift was that Hayek sought to propound that the individual mind did not actually choose the rules that worked the best: that was done either through a sort of quasi-evolutionary selection of life success at the individual level reinforcing the relevant classifier rules or, more frequently, natural selection weeding out the individuals with unfit rules in favor of those individuals lucky enough to come previously equipped with superior classifiers. It was, not to mince words, a harsh version of social Darwinism.

It is important to understand how this refracted the very notion of radical ignorance as a natural state of being for mankind in the later political economy of Hayek.[10] In this conception, the process of coming-to-know became largely disengaged from the knower, with most of the action happening at the subconscious level. As he wrote in his "Primacy of the Abstract," "the formation of a new abstraction seems *never* to be the outcome of a conscious process, not something at which the mind can deliberately aim, but always a discovery of something which *already* guides its operation" (1978, 46). Here, the celebrated philosopher of freedom postulated a grim species of predestination that would make even Calvin blush. The political implication was clear: if an individual mind could not even reliably plan or organize its own pathway of learning through life, it would exhibit contemptible *hubris* to think it could ever plan the lives of others, much less a whole economy. Knowledge here was no longer like entropy, or pixie dust; now it resembled a great submerged iceberg, nine-tenths invisible, and frozen into place aeons ago, with only minor changes around the margins when it jostled up against other similar icebergs.

How did these lumbering monads ever manage to communicate, much less live in societies that displayed any reliable level of organization? That question was finally answered in the third movement of Hayek's Surprise Symphony. Strangely for a doctrine that started out so concerned over respect for the inviolate individual and his or her subjectivity, the late Hayek rendered his system internally coherent by admitting that knowledge did not really persist in the level of the individual mind, for the most part, but was processed and invested with meaning at the suprapersonal level. In a catchphrase, since so much that people actually knew was inaccessible to them, the only entity that really was capable of judging and validating human knowledge was The Market. The key turning point, as Hayek informs us in *The Fatal Conceit,* was his 1968 essay "Competition as a Discovery Procedure":

> [Epistemology is governed by] competition as a procedure for the discovery of such facts as, without resort to it, *would not be known to anyone* . . . The knowledge of which I speak consists rather of a capacity to find out the particular circumstances, which becomes effective *only if the possessors of this knowledge are informed by the market* which kinds of things or services are wanted, and how urgently they are wanted . . . Knowledge that is used [in a market] is that of *all its members*. Ends that it serves are the separate ends of those individuals, in all their variety and contrariness. (1978, 179, 182–83; emphasis added)

No longer was knowledge being treated as an elusive thing by Hayek, scattered about in an inconvenient matter, because in this version not only is much human knowledge unable to be retrieved from within by the individual in question but, indeed, there exists a species of *knowledge not "known" by any individual human being at all.* Here we are cosseted in the realm of Donald Rumsfeld's infamous "unknown unknowns."[11]

> Now what is the message there? The message is that there are no "knowns." There are things we know that we know. There are known unknowns. That is to say there are things that we now know we don't know. But there are also unknown unknowns. There are things we don't know we don't know. So when we do the best we can and we pull all this information together, and we then say well that's basically what we see as the situation, that is really only the known knowns and the known unknowns. (Rumsfeld 2010)

The only recourse of the rational individual in this subpar situation is primarily to acquiesce in the dictates of signals conveyed by The Market, which hint at deeper truths than most humans will ever know.

But what is this depersonalized and deracinated suprahuman knowledge but a new virtual kind of *information*? This, we think, explains Hayek's rather uncharacteristic reversion to replacing the term "knowledge" with "information" in his last work, *Fatal Conceit.* Sometimes, when it came to this ectoplasmic information, the late Hayek lapsed into his scientistic mode, where evolution had winnowed the elusive truth out of human frailty; but other times, he reverted to full religious mystery: "spontaneous order . . . cannot be properly said to have a purpose . . . known to any single person, or relatively small group of persons" (1978, 183). Some latter-day Austrians have argued that entrepreneurs are just "smarter" than any dedicated intellectual, since they are marinated in this information and thus quicker to respond to market signals.[12] Almost by definition, there is no instrument available to mankind to "test" this proposition. As with all the great world religions, the sole and final terminus for the skeptic was to surrender to Faith: The Market as Super Information Processor knows more than we could ever begin to divine.

One might aver that this is an egregiously idiosyncratic trajectory, the ruinous road to the conflation of pervasive ignorance with virtue, something that would never ever be followed by any prudent rational-choice orthodoxy in economics, nor indeed, any scientific thinker whatsoever.[13] The modern economist often claims to like the early Hayek but thinks he or she tends to studiously avoid the later Hayek. We beg to disagree: the historical record is far richer than that.

Orthodox Epistemologies

Nowadays, one can still find economists that maintain at least some vague awareness that the origins of present-day microeconomics had something to do with Cold War politics—though exactly what may elude them. In discussing the history of the highly influential National Science Foundation / Conference on Econometrics and Mathematical Economics (NSF/CEME) Decentralization Series,[14] the Stanford economist (and former series director) Matthew Jackson (2006) said:

> My impression is that the word decentralization [in the title of the conference] reflects the fact that the starting point in many of the problems addressed by the series is that the necessary information starts in a decentralized state . . . I think that perhaps the history of the conference reflects the fact that these systems were viewed as alternatives to centralized or planned economies when the conference series was first funded, during the cold war.

To fill in a few pertinent details: in the 1950s, economists at Cowles had interpreted Hayek as arguing the relative merit of "free markets" over socialism on informational grounds, and found this argument wanting. In a move that would have vast and enduring ramifications for the future of the economics profession, Leonid Hurwicz and an impressive roster of his colleagues at Cowles responded to Hayek's provocations by reconceiving their own task as external evaluation of the informational properties of economic systems, as if from some great height, claiming soon thereafter that these methods could also inform choice among a plethora of "institutions."[15] Consequently, the Cowlesmen eventually rebranded themselves as experts in "organization," a term that assumed brash capacious dimensions so as to cover such varied phenomena as the internal structuring of large firms, the design of cost-plus contracts for the mobilization of industry during wartime, the evaluation of Soviet central-planning algorithms, and the crafting of commercial regulation.

Indeed, the historian Hunter Heyck has described how a fascination with "organization" became conflated with themes of algorithmic reason and analysis of information across the immediate postwar social sciences.[16] With increasing frequency, these self-identified organization theorists (disproportionately concentrated at Purdue, Caltech, Arizona, and Northwestern in the 1970s) began to contemplate designing *new* institutions, ranging from novel legal regimes to "solutions" for public goods provision to the reorganization of entire economies.[17] And in what turned out to be the most significant development for the future of the economic profession, they would eventually also claim an ability to reconstruct individual precursor markets themselves. The Cowles pretensions to evaluate organizations in general thus paved the way to what eventually became known within economics as "market design."

What followed was a massive upheaval in the practice of economics. Since roughly 1980, the profession converged upon a more "constructivist" approach to markets. Where economists once placidly contemplated markets from without, situated in a space detached from their subject matter, so to speak, instead now they are much less disciplined about their doctrines concerning the nature of economic agency, and much more inclined to be found down in the trenches with other participants, engaged in making markets.

It can be difficult for the outsider to perceive just how radically transformative this turn was, due in no small part to some economists' penchant to maintain a public impression of continuity with their previous activities. In an article for the *New York Times,* Hal Varian (2002) notes economists' participation in the design of an increasingly wide variety of institutions, ranging from the provision of electricity, to the assignment of medical residencies, to financial exchanges. Although the title of Varian's article ("Avoiding the Pitfalls When Economics Shifts from Science to Engineering") may suggest to the reader a periodization, it is truer to the spirit of the article to interpret "shift" as "application," something that characterizes all science—similarly, engineers apply ideas from physics to design bridges. In Varian's telling, someone such as Karl Marx is reinterpreted as an "economic engineer" ("Karl Marx . . . also had ideas about economic design that ended disastrously"), which tends to have the effect of diminishing the novelty of recent developments in economics.[18]

But every once and again, some economist will reflect on just how much has changed. Mark Thoma, the well-known author of the blog *Economist's View,* stated:

> Today I was thinking about the fact that I mainly got into economics to understand how the world works, not to do policy or try to use the tools of economics to recommend how to change economic institutions, though economic policy was certainly of interest too. But mostly I just wanted to understand it all, like a kid taking apart a toy to figure out how it works. I was particularly interested in understanding how money functions and what effect changes in the money supply would have on the economy. I have no idea why economics interests me so much, but it does.
>
> But once I got here, I realized the demand was not just to explain what we know and to be honest about what we don't. People want to know how to make economic institutions function better and they turn to economists to tell them how to accomplish that task. (2006)

The only provision we might make here is that most would view the adjective "economic" as redundant. Over the past two decades, articles in major economics journals appeared proclaiming the advent of "engineering economics," "market design," "auction theory for privatization," and the like.

For the present purposes, we take for granted the significance of this development, and pose the question: What, if anything, about design is related to Hayek? One obvious answer is that market design shares with Hayek the view that markets don't exist to allocate given physical resources so much as they serve to integrate and disseminate something called "knowledge." Another would attribute to Hayek the very idea that an economy can be "designed": Hayek sought to study the institutional foundations of the "competitive order," as a prelude to constructing an ideal competitive order. Both answers are true enough, but woefully incomplete. Additionally, we wish to insist that Hayek's work on epistemology has left traces on the substantive features of the two dominant approaches to the economics of market design, which we entitle the Bayes-Nash School and the Experimentalist School, for reasons we will elaborate on presently.

The Bayes-Nash School of Design

This historical origin of this school is located in the work of William Vickrey of Columbia University, winner of the 1994 Bank of Sweden Prize and the namesake of the "Vickrey auction." In a 1960 study, Vickrey noted the "strategic misrepresentation of preferences" might prevent the government from gathering information to construct a social welfare function (Vickrey 1960, 517–19). A year later, he raised a similar concern with the market socialist proposal of Abba Lerner (Vickrey 1961). In his *Economics of Control,* Lerner had proposed a "counterspeculation" method, to be used by a central board to counteract monopolists' (and monopsonists') price-setting power by estimating and guaranteeing a competitive equilibrium price. In other words, Lerner's analysis had suggested to Vickrey that active efforts might be required to gather diffuse information together in one place. In both papers, Vickrey had expressed a novel concern: economists who had hoped to assist the government in gathering dispersed information would encounter a problem. This problem was, in a word, *mendacity*: those holding the crucial information had the capacity to distort it, and for strategic reasons might be expected to do so.

Vickrey responded to this new problem in a way that will by now seem commonplace to the student of economics: he explored the incentive properties of four auction types—the first price and second price sealed bid, the English, and the Dutch auctions—and used Nash game theory to do so. From today's vantage point, it is tempting to become excessively fascinated by Vickrey's appeal to game theory as a generic logic of strategic choice, and consequently to ignore the most significant features of Vickrey's work. For Vickrey's version of epistemology, it was no longer possible to hold tight to one's private information—so long as the analyst crafted a method to get in your head to pry the information out of there.[19]

To do so would require employing one of a handful of "incentive compatible" auctions. We know that this idea would eventually be greeted with much fanfare, but at the time pretty much everyone ignored Vickrey's use of game theory; even Vickrey would downplay its significance, as "one of my digressions into abstract economics, at best of minor significance in terms of human welfare" (Dreze 1998).

It would be left to other scholars sharing Cowles's enthusiasms to make the most significant developments along these lines. The key figure here was Robert Wilson of Stanford's Graduate School of Business who, although not formally affiliated with Cowles or RAND, came to share many of their enthusiasms.[20] Wilson's Stanford department became the first institution devoted to the study of modeling Bayesian actors interacting in markets; along with his students Armando Ortega Reichert, Paul Milgrom, and Peter Cramton, Wilson would form what we call the Bayes-Nash School of Design.[21] The operations researcher Michael Rothkopf was one of the few close observers to put his finger on the true significance of Wilson's innovation:

> Quite recently publications have begun to appear that indicate that operations researchers are starting to construct bidding models that are realistic and that consider simultaneously the optimality of the decisions of all bidders. The new factor taken into consideration in these models is the uncertainty faced by the bidders as to the value of the subject of the auction. In most of this work, the uncertainty of each bidder is restricted to the value of the subject of the auction to his competitors. Only Wilson has begun to take account of the uncertainty of a bidder about the value of the subject of the auction to himself. (Rothkopf 1969, 362)

Agents no longer knew their values—their knowledge could now be *wrong,* and much in need of correction. Economists of the Bayes-Nash tradition would generously offer to help them out.

This correction would take place within the context of an auction game. This school portrays all bidders as viewing the auction game in the same way—the structure of the game is purportedly "common knowledge." Bidding against other bidders immediately raised the specter of having to take competing bidders' beliefs into account, and therefore the complexity of dealing with "beliefs about beliefs." The complex hierarchies of "beliefs about beliefs" are collapsed into a single statistic, dubbed a "type." Initially, I am presumed to know only my own "type," and will assume that I am the same as my opponents (i.e., we are the same "types"). As information is released over the course of the auction, I come to appreciate how my opponents differ from myself. This appreciation matters not only for strategic reasons but also for epistemic reasons: because the roster of types is presumed to be stochastically distributed around a true-valued mean, it is only by participating in an auction that I come to know my own value. How this works can best be understood by considering a typical model of an "English Auction" conducted for a single item for sale.

In an English Auction, the price of the item for sale starts out low and rises until all bidders drop out save one. The lone bidder remaining "wins" the item, and pays an amount equal to the price prevailing at the time the second-to-last bidder dropped out. According to the Bayes-Nash approach, bidders should use the information released by their competitors dropping out of the auction to reconsider and recalibrate their own valuations, and should continue to bid so long as the expected value of winning the auction conditional upon all remaining bidders dropping out is greater than or equal to the price of the good.[22]

Significantly, the informational claims of Hayek were also foremost in the consideration of members of the Bayes-Nash School of Design. Consider Wilson:

> A half-century ago, Friedrich von Hayek offered a new perspective on markets, prices, and the invisible hand. In his view, the fundamental process of a market economy

> is price formation. He interprets prices resulting from competing bids and offers as summaries of information dispersed among traders . . . A quarter-century later, the developers of the Economics of Information discovered that market imperfections attributable to informational asymmetries can cause serious inefficiencies . . . Initially, the main analytical tool was price theory, but more recently it has been game theory. In particular, it is the flavor of game theory that originates in the work of . . . John Harsanyi. (Wilson 1996, 296)

And, in a survey article on the Bayes-Nash School, consider the more specific reference linking a result of the school to the work of Hayek:

> It is often pointed out (for example, by Hayek [in "The Use of Knowledge in Society"]) that one of the remarkable and important features of the price system is its ability to convey information efficiently. All that a buyer or a seller needs to know about a commodity's supply or demand is summarized by a single number, its price. Does the process of price formation by competitive bidding have such information efficiencies? In the common-value model, the bidders lack complete information about the item's true value; each bidder has different partial information. However, even though no single bidder has perfect information, it can be shown that, if there is perfect competition in the bidding, the selling price reflects all of the bidders' private information . . . Thus the selling price conveys information about the item's true value. With perfect competition, the price is equal to the true value even though no individual in the economy knows what this true value is and no communication among the bidders takes place. (McAfee and McMillan 1987, 721–22)

Note well that these leading members of the Bayes-Nash School made reference to the work of Hayek in the context of interpreting the significance of their own achievements. Agents' knowledge was portrayed as difficult to access by the auctioneer/central planner; but it was also difficult for the agents themselves to access: in contrast to the conventional Walrasian view, agents' knowledge was *untrustworthy.* But while agents' knowledge was deemed untrustworthy, they were still able to incorporate more information into their valuations, and therefore were deemed capable of highly sophisticated reasoning. The market would provide the information needed to carry out such sophisticated reasoning.

Now, markets could be enlisted to help agents think. "Truth" was now located both "out there" and "in here"—at least once the market had done its work. Truth was "out there" in that the market was designed in such a way that the price of an appropriately designed auction equaled the putative objective monetary value of an item for sale; it was "in here" in that bidders were sophisticated enough to infer this value from the "signals" conveyed by other bidders during the auction process, avoiding any behavior they would later regret, at least in equilibrium.

The Experimentalist School of Design

Let us first acknowledge the obvious: claiming that experimental economics constitutes a distinct school of market design is likely to strike some contemporaries as rather odd. After all, isn't experimentation about making economics more scientific by subjecting theoretical claims to controlled testing? But experimentalists have harbored far more vaunting ambitions. One gets a sense of these ambitions by examining the backgrounds of Vernon Smith, Charles Plott, Stephen Rassenti, Robert Bulfin, and Alvin Roth. The first thing to notice about this crew is that they did not trace their genealogy out of some well-established social scientific experimental tradition, such as that found in psychology, but instead hailed from engineering and operations research. In light of this background, it begins to make sense that such figures would also occupy themselves with problems of economic design. And then there are additional reasons.

The Experimentalist School of Design has roots in the earlier work of the Walrasian mechanism designers, the development in engineering departments of optimization routines, the development within economic laboratories of computerized experimental methods, and the neoliberal field of "public choice." The first contribution of experimentalists to attract the rapt attention of the orthodoxy (perhaps we should call it experimental economics' "killer app") was *not* the testing of economic theory, but instead the development and deployment of novel market forms to displace bureaucratic decision making. Under the new regime, the market, including its rules and participants, would now be explicitly conceived as a "person-machine system," a hybrid computational device.[23]

Experimentalists nowadays proclaim that everywhere, from the trading pit to the regulator's office to the corporate boardroom, can benefit from a little "economic system design."[24] In one respect, the first adjective is a bit of a misnomer, or at least imprecise, since for modern experimentalists there is no delimited "economy" that serves to circumscribe their attentions; hence, for the Experimentalist School, unlike in the cases of our previous schools, there can be no canonical model of the economy. There is, however, a generic "set packing problem" that results in complications that must be addressed in order to successfully design an economic system. The distinctive mathematical feature of this maximization problem is that because bids for packages are permitted, solving the maximization problem involves properly assigning prices to disjoint sets of items.

One feature of this approach is an intensified and more sophisticated focus on the algorithmic properties of the market than previously available.[25] When stressing the computational properties of market operations, these market designers appeal to the "computational efficiency" of algorithms. When focusing on the algorithmic properties of markets, this approach recommends substituting less computationally burdensome procedures, often by shifting part—though not very much—of the computational burden onto the "human persons" (bidders, in the case of markets) to assist in the search process (Porter et al. 2003, 11154). Markets, once conflated with the act of exchange, are now credited with being able to solve immensely complex maximization problems of any provenance. The relative status of humans versus "mechanisms" in this process becomes inverted in the quest to overcome complexity.

Although they did talk about offloading some of the computational burden onto agents, market designers did not view the "person" part of this "person-machine system" with much in the way of cognitive capacity. Perhaps some of this attitude derived from the experience of manipulating students in experimental settings. The dreaded hive mind of collective consciousness had finally made its appearance in economics. Agents are shape-shifters; sometimes viewed as incapable of coping with the substantial computational requirements imposed on them by Bayesian inference; in some other cases they can't think at all. People may be smart, stupid, or anywhere in between in the New New Economics. But prudence dictates it is best to assume the worst, and to ensure that the performance of markets is robust to the cognitive capacities of agents, or lack thereof. Such robustness is accomplished by offloading most of the task of information processing entirely onto the market mechanisms. The economist's task is now to build markets to handle the cognition that agents cannot—or, to use the highly appropriate term favored by experimentalists, to build "smart markets."

Experimentalists also framed their interventions by referring to the ideas of Hayek. One observes such framing in experimentalists' activities in making smart markets:

> The objective is to combine the information advantages of decentralized ownership with the coordination advantages of central processing . . . In effect we offer a solution to the Lange-Lerner-Hayek controversy of the 1930s. (V. Smith 1991, 811)

In discussing "information advantages," the importance of "central processing" is paramount. Central processing enables the completion of trades too complicated for individuals to complete on their own: "There is a puzzle as to the processes whereby our brains have [market exchange] and other skills so deeply hidden from our calculating self-aware minds" (V. Smith 2010, 5). At the hands of the Experimentalist School, the market is redescribed as a "price discovery" process, in almost direct parallel to Hayek's late discussion of competition as a discovery process. For example, Charles Plott titled the second volume of his collected papers *Market Institutions and Price Discovery* and characterized the lessons emerging from the work comprising a substantial part of the volume as follows:

> It is focused on the mysterious process through which markets find price. From Vernon Smith's early discovery of the ability of the law of supply and demand to predict price, the mechanism that produces the market price has been a mystery. In many senses the market operates like a set of computers, operating in parallel to compute the equilibrium price, which is unknown to everyone in the market before the market produces the answer. In this sense, the concept of "price discovery" as it is used in the work of market-makers is appropriate. (Plott 2001, xxiv)

The change in language reflects the Experimentalist view that only skillfully designed markets—"smart markets"—can find the economic knowledge that cognitively limited agents are *incapable* of knowing. This view is highly compatible with the notion that markets have the power to know things that agents cannot, the position taken by Hayek during his third period:

> In a 1968 lecture, "Competition as a Discovery Procedure," Hayek says ". . . I propose to consider competition as a procedure for the discovery of such facts as . . . (otherwise) would not be known to anyone . . ." Great insight; experiments have long demonstrated Hayek's

> proposition. People discover a price that they didn't know existed. (V. Smith 2015, 242)

And in direct reference to the ability of skillfully defined markets to substitute for human cognition:

> Human interactive experiments governed by a computer network enabled the accommodation of far larger message spaces, opened the way to the application of coordination and optimization algorithms to the messages of subjects, and facilitated their capacity to reach sophisticated equilibrium outcomes they did not need to understand. (V. Smith 2006, xii)

Economic designers had managed to convince themselves that they had faithfully come to grips with Hayek's concerns.[26] The early Cowles-based designers viewed themselves as assisting the government in a number of areas—proposing planning rules and suggesting the information to gather. Agents knew their "private" information, but the government did not. This established for them the task of "rational design of the institutional framework," which would amount to a novel kind of economic-cum-communication system—not central planning, but not quite like the market, either. Initially, economists conceived themselves as designing various methods to help gather information; knowledge was held by dispersed agents, and the job of the economic designer was to figure out how best to transport knowledge from where it was to where it wasn't—lest the economy not operate properly. Designers of the Bayes-Nash School tasked themselves with helping agents to come to know *their own* values. This they would do by helping agents to correctly infer values, then by recommending the use of knowledge-enhancing auction forms. In an environment where economists increasingly found themselves selling their expertise, such ambitions carried considerable appeal. Although game theorists attributed immensely impressive prodigious rationality to the agent, nevertheless economists managed to carve out a special role for their own activities. Finally, the Experimentalist School viewed the task of designers as constructing machines to discover knowledge that individuals could not discover or otherwise comprehend themselves. These "smart markets" would include people, but in practice would substitute for the judgment of people—for example, by replacing regulatory bureaucracies. The Ghost of Hayek haunted them all.

Organizational Possibilities for Our Grandchildren

Over the past twenty years, economists of all stripes have found themselves engaged in the provision of boutique markets, deployed for a variety of purposes.[27] The economist is now just an engineer, as Noah Smith put it, and engineers qua engineers don't do politics: they just want the bridge to hold. Of course, Vernon Smith and Charles Plott make for uncomfortable counterexamples to this position, given that they are card-carrying MPS members and wear their politics on their sleeves. But for economists who herald the engineering turn, neither Smith nor Plott is the first one to come to mind.[28]

That nonideological personage would be 2012 Bank of Sweden prizewinner Alvin Roth. Roth's renown comes not merely or even primarily from exercises in theorem proving, or in devising a set of protocols for subjecting some proposition to a controlled empirical test (though he certainly has done both). Instead, to quote the Bank of Sweden's press release upon the announcement of his prize, his recognition comes from "the practice of market design," including the development of "systems for matching doctors with hospitals, school pupils with schools, and organ donors with patients" (Nobel Media AB 2014). To the public, Roth is often held out as the exemplary new model economist: the most visible face of a profession that leverages expertise not to advance an ideology, but to engineer ingenious practical solutions to difficult and important problems.

Because these solutions must actually work in the real world, ideologues need not apply. In a blog post entitled "Not all economists are neoliberal, honest," Diane Coyle voices this attitude perfectly:

> Where it is appropriate to prioritize efficiency, or to use market processes to achieve either efficiency or other outcomes, should always be a matter of public and political debate. Most of the economists I hang out with—applied micro people—think it will depend on both people's political choices and on the exact circumstances: the US trade in S02 emissions works well, the EU market in carbon emissions does not; Alvin Roth's matching markets for kidneys or medical jobs are magical (and no money changes hands). My kind of economists tend to be pragmatists, unlike those in politics who argue the market is always best. (Coyle 2015)[29]

Recent years have seen the term "freshwater versus saltwater" recycled for public use, yet no one would think to suggest that Roth belonged to either camp: upon his receipt of the Bank of Sweden Prize, "freshwater" and "saltwater" alike heaped praise on Roth's work (see, for example, Levitt 2012). Among the Micro, Roth assumed a nearly unparalleled stature: after posing the question "What is market design?" one well-respected game theorist quipped (only partly in jest), "Whatever Alvin Roth says it is" (Vohra 2014). If ever there were a person who could wrest market design from the "bad Hayek," it would be Roth.

All of which makes Roth's discussions of Hayek so noteworthy. In his much-lauded post- prize book-length popularization of his work, *Who Gets What—and Why,* Roth links market design to Hayek in the following way:

> I made the analogy between a free market with effective rules and a wheel that can rotate freely because it has an axle and well-oiled bearings. I could have been paraphrasing the iconic free-market economist Friedrich Hayek . . . He understood that markets need effective rules to work

> freely. Hayek also understood that there is a place for economists to help in understanding how to design markets . . . Debates about markets often use the phrase "free markets" as a slogan, sometimes as if markets work best without any rules other than property rights. Hayek had something to say about that, too: "Probably nothing has done so much harm to the liberal cause as the wooden insistence of some liberals on certain rules of thumb, above all the principle of laissez faire." (Roth 2015, 226–27)

We take this passage not as some smoking-gun evidence that Roth intended to set out to craft a high-tech Hayekianism, but rather as providing some indication of how pervasive neoliberal ideas are. From these words, one can almost sense Roth's surprise upon picking up Hayek for the first time and finding so much of what he said to be so amenable to his own views: Hayek was opposed to laissez faire, held that markets are constructed entities, and that careful attention must be paid to institutional structure. So, too, for Roth.[30]

The reader might well think of Roth's words here as indicative of nothing more than a recognition in Hayek's work of constructivist and informational themes, with none of the attendant epistemology, or certainly his politics. It is, after all, a good distance between the design of a clearinghouse for medical residents and, say, articulating a rationale for authoritarian liberalism or, more to the point, designing a constitution. Hence, we are fortunate that Alvin Roth has also speculated in print on a variety of political and economic matters—the occasion for which was his participation in a volume wherein "leading economists" were asked to speculate on what the world will look like in 100 years (Palacios-Huerta 2014). While the recent performance of the economics profession should inspire no confidence whatsoever in the predictions of its members, closely reading Roth's fantasies can give insight into the state of economics today.

At first glance, Roth's essay might strike one as the musings of an engineer who is optimistic in his estimation of humanity's ability to answer the "big questions" facing it, but humble in the role he reserves for economists in providing the answers. Indeed, Roth favorably quotes Keynes's famous passage from "Economic Possibilities for Our Grandchildren," wherein Keynes counseled that economists accept this kind of role: "If economists could manage to get themselves thought of as humble, competent people, on a level with dentists, that would be splendid!" Roth then adds, "Perhaps if we replace *dentists* with *engineers,* that is still a good goal for the next hundred years" (Roth 2014, 119). And yet, Roth's engineer-economist is entrusted with far more than routine cleanings, filling cavities, or the occasional root canal. According to Roth:

> As computers and computer science continue to advance, artificial intelligence will have crossed the barrier so that some parts of technology will be self-directing—able to operate not merely without direct human supervision but able to formulate intermediate goals as well as plans of action to achieve them . . . As computer assistance becomes more ubiquitous in all aspects of life, some of that assistance will be in markets, helping us piece together things we need . . . without the time-consuming personal attention that some person would have to give to the task. (Roth 2014, 117)

No longer will the market necessarily give people what they say they want—instead it is designed to operate regardless of their wants. An ever-increasing amount of thinking will be offloaded onto smart markets, which will then be commodified and sold. Some of market design will be deskilled, but no matter because the unbounded scope of "design economics" will offer inexhaustible opportunities for the economist-engineer. According to Roth:

> Computerized markets will make market design more important, as many market details will have to be embodied in computer code. But many kinds of market design that are today crafted by specialists will have passed from frontier knowledge to whatever is then the equivalent of

> shrink-wrapped software, much the way that techniques of mathematical optimization that once were the domain of PhDs in operations research have become available in software packages. But there will still be unsolved problems of organization and coordination, so market design (or, more generally, design economics dealing not just with markets but with the design of all forms of organizing, transacting, and allocating) will have become and will remain an important part of economics. (Roth 2014, 117–18)

But the future is now. As we noted in the previous section, economists, beginning with those at Cowles but rapidly spreading outward, have styled themselves as experts in the design of organizations for at least four decades. And, indeed, returning to *Who Gets What,* Roth offers the following *present* account of market design: "Successful designs depend greatly on the details of the market, including the culture and psychology of the participants" (Roth 2015, 78). And, more specifically, "if you really want to operate at digital speeds, you need to take people out of the middle of the process" (Roth 2015, 101). This is *today's* reality: the market is a person-machine system, with the thinking offloaded onto things. If anything has changed, it is the scope of the economists' ambitions.

When listing all the domains and stuff of modern social life that could be conceptualized as markets, Roth works himself into a frenzy:

> Amazon couldn't have become the marketplace it is without the Internet, which couldn't have become a marketplace without first computers and then smartphones. And smartphones couldn't have become marketplaces without a way to pay for purchases over the phone . . . On the Internet, it's convenient to pay with a credit card. And a credit card is also a marketplace . . . [M]arkets include not only our experiences at the supermarket or phone store but also those in getting into college, finding a job, eating

> breakfast—even getting a kidney transplant. (Roth 2015, 22–23, 27)

In Roth's vision, markets will have spread into every nook and cranny of human existence: reproduction will be commodified and separated from sexual intercourse; performance-enhancing drugs will become as common as milk for children and coffee for adults; parents will fork out big bucks to purchase better genetic endowments for their children.

Although Roth does acknowledge that some of these developments might make the present day reader squeamish, this too shall pass, as future generations will come to marvel at why anyone ever thought purchasing organs was a big deal. More to the point, such squeamishness becomes just another topic of study for the market designer, who casts an unsentimental eye upon "repugnant transactions," and sets to the task of creating workarounds. Roth's "100 years" essay serves less as prognostication than as a window into the thinking of the present-day market designer, for which everything becomes a market—down to the very quiddity of the self.

Market design was the unintended consequence of orthodox economists grappling with themes introduced by Hayek. None of the preceding should be taken to suggest that neoliberals concocted market design, only to impose it upon unsuspecting economists, thereby foisting neoliberalism upon them. Indeed, not all card-carrying neoliberal economists liked what they saw. To take but one example, in Roth's Bank of Sweden lecture (Roth 2012), Roth tweaked George Stigler, who in his capacity as editor of the *Journal of Political Economy* rejected early work of Roth on market design as "not economics." For the most part, though, neoliberals came around. They have wanted to link their prescriptions to the most recent ideas about how markets work, and those ideas have fit neoliberal politics to a "T".

Slowly at first, but then with astonishing rapidity, the aspirations of economists and policymakers converged on the task of thoroughly redesigning the organizations of the economic lifeworld from bottom to top. Market designers offered to lend their expertise (for a price), and with increasing frequency policymakers took them up on their offer. This convergence was no accident. Policymaker and economist alike came to appreciate how real-world markets came to increasingly resemble information processors, and adjusted their aspirations in light of this; both would come to attribute immense epistemic capacities to these markets. As a practical matter, this justified the piecemeal marketization of government functions and ultimately full privatization; as a theoretical matter, this served to degrade the cognitive capacities of the agent. Market design turned out to be a perfect "fit" for its time, because it constitutes the precepts of neoliberalism taken to their logical conclusion.[31]

Now The Market is not merely an information processor but an *omnipotent* processor of information: That Than Which No Greater Can Be Conceived. Markets are somehow both more transparent than bureaucracy and yet their design is both too important a matter and too opaque to leave to democratic deliberation, since the democratic public is incapable of comprehending the operation of markets. As market participants, people are regarded as the weak link in this complex technology, their severe cognitive limitations a clear threat to its proper functioning. Consequently, markets are less and less conceived as being about giving people what they may think they want, and increasingly about operating regardless of their wants. Here one finds the terminus of Hayek's struggles with epistemology, with the full neoliberalization of information economics.

These "markets" of the market designers were *not* the markets of yore. They might, like conventional markets, rely on prices; but then again, like Roth's kidney exchanges (and Cowlesian central-planning schemes), they might not. Yet nor were they exactly the same as older structures of bureaucracy. They were something else altogether: immensely complex algorithmic procedures, instantiated through the process of *bricolage,* and offered in the spirit of substituting a "reliable" technology of governance for methods that previously had unfortunately depended on the woefully unreliable human element. Consequently, anywhere humans gathered to resolve anything—the regulatory committee hearing, obviously, but also the voting booth and the corporate boardroom—lurking was a candidate for market design. It was the most ambitious program in the history of economics: petitioning to repeal the Corn Laws, installing a Pigouvian tax, engaging in a bit of macroeconomic fine-tuning, or even thoroughgoing economy-wide central planning appear quaint by comparison. Market designers offered to assume responsibility for reconstructing the nature of Society from top to bottom.

Notes

1. For initial responses to the award, see Boettke (2007) and Tabbarok (2007). For one example of a paper devoted to establishing Hayek's influence on the neoclassical orthodoxy, see Skarbek (2009).
2. Regarding the former, see Boettke (2002). Regarding the latter, see Lavoie (1986).
3. Here and there one encounters the claim that game theory should be viewed as an outgrowth of a broader Austrian tradition, yet such claims are advanced halfheartedly and without reference to Hayek's work. See Foss (2000) and Kiesling (2015).
4. The roster of invitees to the George Mason conference included Israel Kirzner, Edmund Phelps, Vernon Smith, as well as Maskin—which gives some indication of the insights that can be expected from this project.
5. Pride of place goes to Oguz (2010); other useful sources are Kahlil (2002), Lavoie (1985), and Boettke and O'Donnell (2013).
6. The prehistory of neoliberalism growing out of Weberian sociology has been the subject of recent intensive research by Nick Gane (see Ossandón 2014).
7. It may not be amiss to point out this structural similarity to Shannon's use of entropy was one reason the Hayekian "first movement" proved so popular well outside the professional precincts of economics, as in artificial intelligence.
8. On the structure of associationist psychology, see Daston (1978) and Mandelbaum (2015).
9. It has not been clear to subsequent commentators just how different, and even opposed, were Polanyi's and Hayek's philosophies of knowledge. This has been occluded by assertions that they both believed in similar notions of "tacit knowledge." On this, see Mirowski (1998), Oguz (2010), Bateira (in Dolfsma and Soete 2006), and Butos (2010). Nevertheless, the Hayekian version of unconscious rationality was popularized for noneconomists in Gladwell (2005).

10 See Boettke and O'Donnell (2013, 314): "Radical ignorance is a significant element of Hayek's economic thought."

11 Rumsfeld was himself a member in good standing of the neoliberal thought collective, an avowed acolyte of Milton Friedman. For the quote, see Rumsfeld (2010). It has been reported that Donald Rumsfeld, in a speech at Milton Friedman's ninetieth birthday party in 2002, held by the Bush White House to honor Friedman's legacy, said, "Milton [Friedman] is the embodiment of the truth that ideas have consequences."

12 See, for instance, Diamond (2012).

13 Cowan, David, and Foray propose a similar taxonomy—articulated, unarticulated, and inarticulable knowledge—without citing Hayek, only to reject the third category as "not very interesting for the social sciences" (2000, 230). This paper shows just how misguided their judgment was.

14 The NSF/CEME series ran yearly; its roster of participants included nearly every major figure in postwar microeconomics.

15 "The comparative merits of alternative systems are typically being debated under such labels as centralization against decentralization, social control or planning against free markets, or in similar terms. This dichotomy was present in the famous Mises-Hayek-Lange-Lerner controversy concerning the feasibility of socialism . . . A survey of the literature will show that issues concerning the proper internal structure of business and other large organizations involves *[sic]* similar dichotomies" (Hurwicz 1971, 80). For a recollection of this work, see Reiter (2009).

16 He associates what he calls "high modern social science" with "an abiding interest in the means by which systems store, process, and communicate information about themselves and their environments, often expressed through the formal analysis of information" (Heyck 2015, 11).

17 "Problems of economic policy may be grouped in two broad classes which may be loosely described as those involving choice of the value of a 'parameter' within a given system of economic institutions and those involving choice among institutions . . . Examples of the second type include the design of 'new' economic systems, such as were embodied in the Yugoslav economic reform of 1968" (Mount and Reiter 1974, 161).

18 Varian's career may be taken as a better indicator of the profession's changes. Formerly a professor at University of California, Berkeley, and a well-known writer of a widely read graduate textbook in microeconomics, Varian now serves as chief economist for Google.

19 According to Roger Myerson, Vickrey had produced "the one great paper with a truly modern treatment of information before Harsanyi" (2004, 1818).

20 One example of this shared enthusiasm is Wilson's contribution to the study of "decentralization under uncertainty" (Wilson 1969b). For his contributions to Social Choice Theory, see Wilson (1969a; 1969c).

21 Interestingly, Alvin Roth would also study under Wilson. We discuss the work of Roth in more detail below. Later, the center of gravity shifted to Northwestern

University, as the program initiated there by Stanley Reiter came to house an increasing number of game theorists.

22 Milgrom and Weber (1982) is generally regarded as providing the canonical model of the Bayes-Nash approach (Krishna 2002, 83–102; McMillan 1994, 146).

23 One of us has discussed this development in a different context as a shift of economics into the realm of the "cyborg sciences" (Mirowski 2002).

24 During the period it was the epicenter of studies in experimental economics, George Mason University established a graduate certification in economic system design; today, Chapman University (home to Vernon Smith) offers an MS in economic system design.

25 "Mechanism design has matured over the past 20 years by focusing on incentive compatibility and political viability. The analysis has usually been carried out under the working assumption that infinite computing capacity is always available. Any computation required of the individuals or of the system can be instantaneously and correctly completed. Of course, any expert in organizational computing knows this is clearly wrong" (Ledyard 1993, 122). Ledyard devoted the rest of his article to suggesting how to bring together research in organizational computing and the economics of market design.

26 As we have seen, they failed to convince many Austrians of the same, at least regarding the activities of the Walrasian and Bayes-Nash Schools. Their reactions to the design activities of the experimentalists have been more muted, possibly because of formal affiliation with the neoliberal project: both Vernon Smith and Charles Plott are members of the Mont Pèlerin Society.

27 Although this is not the place to rehearse the argument in its entirety, a strong case can be made that the history displays a pronounced tendency in the direction of what we have called the "Experimentalist School of Design" (see Mirowski and Nik-Khah 2017).

28 Characteristically, Noah Smith seems to miss even this point, assuming instead that Smith's belief that markets can generate asset bubbles disqualifies him as a "market-oriented thinker" (N. Smith 2015).

29 See also Hal Varian's (2002) discussion of Roth's work in the *New York Times.*

30 Moreover, Roth makes use of the language of "price discovery," though he tends to waver between the epistemic views of the game theorists and the experimentalists (see, esp. Roth 2015, 185–88).

31 Although we tend to forget it now, pioneers in this effort often wore their neoliberal commitments on their sleeve. For example, Charles Plott credited his work in design to MPS member James Buchanan's "constitutional political economy" (see Lee 2015).

References

Boettke, Peter. 2002. "Information and Knowledge: Austrian Economics in Search of Its Uniqueness." *Review of Austrian Economics* 15, no. 4: 263–74.

Boettke, Peter. 2007. "A Market Nobel." *The Wall Street Journal*, October 16.

Boettke, Peter, and Christopher Coyne. 2015. "Hayek's Nobel after 40 Years." *Review of Austrian Economics* 28, no. 3: 221–23.

Boettke, Peter, and Kyle O'Donnell. 2013. "The Failed Appropriation of F. A. Hayek by Formalist Economics." *Critical Review* 25, no. 3–4: 305–41.

Butos, William. 2010. *The Social Science of Hayek's Sensory Order.* Bingley, UK: Emerald Group.

Cowan, Robin, Paul David, and Dominique Foray. 2000. "The Explicit Economics of Knowledge: Codification and Tacitness." *Industrial and Corporate Change* 9, no. 2: 211–53.

Coyle, Diane. 2015. "Not All Economists Are Neoliberal, Honest." *The Enlightened Economist,* July 18. Accessed October 16, 2016. http://www.enlightenmenteconomics.com/blog/index.php/2015/07/not-all-economists-are-neoliberal-honest/.

Daston, Lorraine. 1978. "British Responses to Psycho-Physiology, 1860–1900." *Isis* 69, no. 2: 192–208.

Diamond, Arthur. 2012. "The Epistemology of Entrepreneurship." *Advances in Austrian Economics* 17:111–42.

Dolfsma, Wilfred, and Luc Soete, eds. 2006. *Understanding the Dynamics of a Knowledge Economy.* Cheltenham, UK: Elgar.

Dreze, Jacques. 1998. "William S. Vickrey, 1914–1996." *National Academy of Sciences Biographical Memoirs.* Washington DC: National Academies Press. Accessed 16 October, 2016. http://www.nasonline.org/publications/biographical-memoirs/memoir-pdfs/vickrey-william.pdf.

Foss, Nicolai. 2000. "Austrian Economics and Game Theory: A Stocktaking and an Evaluation." *Review of Austrian Economics* 13, no. 1: 41–58.

Gladwell, Malcolm. 2005. *Blink: The Power of Thinking without Thinking.* New York: Little Brown.

Hayek, Friedrich. 1945. "The Use of Knowledge in Society." *American Economic Review* 35, no. 4: 519–30.

Hayek, Friedrich. 1952. *The Sensory Order.* Chicago: University of Chicago Press.

Hayek, Friedrich. 1978. *New Studies in Philosophy, Politics, Economics, and the History of Ideas.* London: Routledge.

Hayek, Friedrich. 1988. *The Fatal Conceit.* Chicago: University of Chicago Press.

Heyck, Hunter. 2015. *The Age of System.* Baltimore: The Johns Hopkins University Press.

Hurwicz, Leonid. 1971. "Centralization and Decentralization in Economic Processes." In *Comparison of Economic Systems,* edited by A. Eckstein, 79–102. Berkeley: University of California Press.

Jackson, Matthew. 2006. "Background on the NSF/CEME Decentralization Conference Series." *Stanford.Edu.* Last modified July 20, 2016. http://web.stanford.edu/~jacksonm/history.htm.

Khalil, Elias. 2002. "Information, Knowledge, and the Close of Friedrich Hayek's System." *Eastern Economic Journal* 28, no. 3: 319–41.

Kiesling, Lynne. 2015. "The Knowledge Problem." In *Oxford Handbook of Austrian Economics,* edited by P. Boettke, 45–64. Oxford: Oxford University Press.

Krishna, Vijay. 2002. *Auction Theory.* San Diego: Academic Press.

Lavoie, Don. 1985. *Rivalry and Central Planning.* New York: Cambridge University Press.

Lavoie, Don. 1986. "The Market as a Procedure for Discovery and Conveyance of Inarticulate Knowledge." *Comparative Economic Studies* 28, no. 1: 1–19.

Ledyard, John. 1993. "The Design of Coordination Mechanisms and Organizational Computing." *Journal of Organizational Computing* 3, no. 1: 121–34.

Lee, Kyu Sang. 2015. "Mechanism Designers in Alliance: A Portrayal of a Scholarly Network in Support of Experimental Economics." Working Paper.

Levitt, Steven D. 2012. "Al Roth Takes Home the Nobel Prize." *Freakonomics,* October 15. Accessed October 16, 2016. http://freakonomics.com/2012/10/15/al-roth-takes-home-the-nobel-prize/.

Mandelbaum, Eric. 2015. "Associationist Theories of Thought." *Stanford Encyclopedia of Philosophy*. Accessed October 16, 2016. http://plato.stanford.edu/entries/associationist-thought/.

Maskin, Eric. 2015. "Friedrich von Hayek and Mechanism Design." *Review of Austrian Economics* 28, no. 3: 247–52.

McAfee, R. P., and John McMillan. 1987. "Auctions and Bidding." *Journal of Economic Literature* 25, no. 2: 699–738.

McMillan, John. 1994. "Selling Spectrum Rights." *Journal of Economic Perspectives* 8, no. 3: 145–62.

Milgrom, Paul, and Robert Weber. 1982. "A Theory of Auctions and Competitive Bidding." *Econometrica* 50, no. 5: 1089–122.

Mirowski, Philip. 1998. "Economics, Science, and Knowledge: Polanyi vs. Hayek." *Tradition and Discovery: The Polanyi Society Periodical* 25, no. 1: 29–42.

Mirowski, Philip. 2002. *Machine Dreams.* New York: Cambridge University Press.

Mirowski, Philip, and Edward Nik-Khah. 2008. "Command Performance: Exploring what STS Thinks It Takes to Build a Market." In *Living in a Material World: Economic Sociology Meets Science and Technology Studies,* ed. Trevor Pinch and Richard Swedberg, 89–128. Cambridge, Mass.: MIT Press.

Mirowski, Philip, and Edward Nik-Khah. 2017. *The Knowledge We Have Lost in Information*. Oxford: Oxford University Press.

Mount, Kenneth and Stanley Reiter. 1974. "The Informational Size of Message Spaces." *Journal of Economic Theory* 8, no. 2: 161–92.

Myerson, Roger. 2004. "Comments on 'Games with Incomplete Information Played by Bayesian Players, I-III'." *Management Science* 50, no. 12S: 1818–24.

Nobel Media AB. 2014. "Alvin E. Roth—Facts." *Nobelprize.org*. Last revised December 2, 2016. http://www.nobelprize.org/nobel_prizes/economic-sciences/laureates/2012/roth-facts.html.

Oguz, Fuat. 2010. "Hayek on Tacit Knowledge." *Journal of Institutional Economics* 6, no. 2: 145–66.

Ossandón, José. 2014. "Is Neoliberalism Weberian? An Interview with Nicholas Gane." *Estudios De La Economía*. Accessed October 16, 2016. https://estudiosdelaeconomia.wordpress.com/2014/09/14/is-neoliberalism-weberian-an-interview-with-nicholas-gane/.

Palacios-Huerta, Ignacio, ed. 2014. *In 100 Years: Leading Economists Predict the Future.* Cambridge, Mass.: MIT Press.

Plott, Charles. 2001. *Market Institutions and Price Discovery*. Northampton, Mass.: Edward Elgar.

Porter, David, Stephen Rassenti, Anil Roopnarine, and Vernon Smith. 2003. "Combinatorial Auction Design." *Proceedings of the National Academy of Sciences* 100, no. 19: 11153–57.

Reiter, Stanley. 2009. "Two Topics in Leo Hurwicz's Research," *Review of Economic Design* 13, no. 1: 3–6.

Roth, Alvin. 2012. "Alvin E. Roth—Biographical." *Nobelprize.org.* Last revised February 20, 2016. http://www.nobelprize.org/nobel_prizes/economic- sciences/laureates /2012/roth-bio.html.

Roth, Alvin. 2014. "In 100 Years." In *In 100 Years: Leading Economists Predict the Future,* edited by Ignacio Palacios-Huerta, 109–19. Cambridge, Mass.: MIT Press.

Roth, Alvin. 2015. *Who Gets What—and Why.* New York: Houghton Mifflin Harcourt.

Rothkopf, Michael. 1969. "A Model of Rational Competitive Bidding." *Management Science* 15, no. 7: 362–73.

Rumsfeld, Donald 2010. "Press Conference at NATO HQ NATO Speeches." Accessed October 19, 2016. http://www.nato.int/docu/speech/2002/s020606g.htm.

Skarbek, David. 2009. "F. A. Hayek's Influence on Nobel Prize Winners." *Review of Austrian Economics* 22: 109–12.

Smith, Noah. 2014a. "Why Economics Gets a Bad Rap." *The Week.* January 15.

Smith, Noah. 2014b. "Economists Used to Be the Priests of Free Markets—Now They're Just a Bunch of Engineers." *qz.com.* Accessed October 26, 2016. http:// qz.com/208402/economics-can-do-many-things-but-it-cannot-help-the-economy/.

Smith, Noah. 2015 "Sci-jacking." *Noahpinion,* January 9. Accessed October 16, 2016. http://noahpinionblog.blogspot.de/2015/01/sci-jacking.html.

Smith, Vernon. 1991. *Papers in Experimental Economics.* New York: Cambridge University Press.

Smith, Vernon. 2006. "Forward." In *Combinatorial Auctions,* edited by Peter Cramton, Yoav Shoham, and Richard Steinberg, xi–xv. Cambridge, Mass.: MIT Press.

Smith, Vernon. 2010. "Theory and Experiment: What Are the Questions?" *Journal of Economic Behavior and Organization* 73, no. 1: 3–15.

Smith, Vernon. 2015. "Discovery Processes, Science, and 'Knowledge-how': Competition as a Discovery Procedure in the Laboratory." *Review of Austrian Economics* 28, no. 3: 237–45.

Solow, Robert. 2012. "Hayek, Friedman, and the Illusions of Conservative Economics." *New Republic,* November 16.

Tabbarok, Alex. 2007. "What Is Mechanism Design?" *Reason.com.* Accessed October 16, 2016. https://reason.com/archives/2007/10/16/what-is-mechanism -design.

Thoma, Mark. 2006. "Economists as Engineers." *Economist's View.* Accessed October 16, 2016. http://economistsview.typepad.com/economistsview/2006/09/econo mists_as_e.html.

Varian, Hal. 2002. "Avoiding the Pitfalls When Economics Shifts grom Science to Engineering." *New York Times,* Aug 29, 2002.

Vickrey, William. 1960. "Utility, Strategy, and Social Decision Rules." *Quarterly Journal of Economics* 74, no. 4: 507–35.

Vickrey, William. 1961. "Counterspeculation, Auctions, and Competitive Sealed Tenders." *Journal of Finance* 16, no. 1: 8–37.

Vohra, Rakesh. 2014. "Market Design Class (Lecture #1)." *The Leisure of the Theory Class,* January 22. Accessed October 16, 2016. https://theoryclass.wordpress.com/2014/01/22/market-design-class-lecture-1/.

Wilson, Robert. 1969a. "Arrow's Possibility Theorem for Vote Trading." In *Mathematical Theory of Committees and Elections,* 26–39. Vienna: Institute for Advanced Studies.

Wilson, Robert. 1969b. "The Role of Uncertainty and the Value of Logrolling in Collective Choice Processes." In *La Decision: Agregation et Dynamique des Ordres de Preference,* edited by Georges Guilbaud, 309–15. Paris: Centre National de la Recherche Scientifique.

Wilson, Robert. 1969c. "The Structure of Incentives for Decentralization under Uncertainty." In *La Decision: Agregation et Dynamique des Ordres de Preference*, edited by Georges Guilbaud, 287–307. Paris: Centre National de la Recherche Scientifique.

Wilson, Robert. 1996. "John Harsanyi and the Economics of Information." *Games and Economic Behavior* 14, no. 2: 296-8.

[3]

Money Determines Our Situation

Jens Schröter

"Media determine our situation" (Kittler 1999, xxxix). This famous statement of Friedrich Kittler, which was the first sentence of his well-known book *Gramophone Film Typewriter* in 1986, was also the first sentence of the introduction to the conference in Lüneburg in summer 2015, on which this text is based. In German media studies today, it is no longer a widely shared premise, since there is a general trend toward praxeology or "the practice turn."[1] Although it is interesting and important to analyze media practices, the radicalization of this praxeological turn tends to erase the genuine contribution of the media themselves, their own dynamics, affordances, and scripts around which media studies ought to be centered. In praxeological studies media are all too often explicitly or implicitly reduced to neutral tools for the practices of human actors or to neutral channels for human intentions—exactly the instrumental conception of media criticized by media theory from its very inception (as my reading of Callon will show). If media were neutral they would be transparent, would have no significance of their own, and would therefore not be worth studying at all.

Of course media archaeology, that is, Kittler's technocentric approach, was criticized for its technodeterminism, if one understands this term as the idea that technologies determine human practices in the strict sense. But I doubt that Kittler ever made this argument. To me, it seems that the nonneutrality of media is in fact already a very simple logical fact. To say: "The technological medium of photography doesn't determine which kinds of photos people in diverse practices want to make" is of course correct. But without photography people wouldn't want to make photographs in the first place. They couldn't even think of doing so. They couldn't even discuss the potentials and limits of their photographic practices. Logically, the medium predates any practice. To say "There is no such thing as photography, but only different photographic practices" is simply nonsensical (I will come back to that "praxeocentric fallacy" later), because how can you identify the practices for your study if you don't already have a notion of photography in mind; a notion that has to be centered in some way or another around a *differentia specifica* of photography in the first place?

To say that media determine our situation first of all means that our situation is different when a medium exists. With regard to digital technologies this actually doesn't say much, because digital technologies are by definition programmable and have to be formed by a situation to be anything whatsoever. But even this shows: although digital computing technologies might be widely programmable (within the limits of what is calculable at all and in reasonable time), their programmability as such can again be seen as a specific script. And that script means that situations become sedimented and determine future situations (see Schröter 2004). It seems that there are media with flexible and with less flexible scripts. But be that as it may in detail, I just want to insist that media cannot be understood as neutral—even if they appear transparent from time to time.

This is especially important when we turn to a medium that seems to be, on the one hand, neutral to the extreme. That is, of course, money (if we can agree that it is a medium).[2] Money seems to be extremely neutral because it can substitute everything—at least in principle. On the other hand, the idea that media determine our situation seems in no case truer than in the case of money: "Money determines our situation." Take a conference as an example: Of course money doesn't determine the topic, the structure, or the personnel of the conference (although people with too expensive flights might be excluded from attending), but its pure existence of course depends on the availability of money. Seen in this way, money is nonneutral to the extreme. It is not just a neutral tool or a neutral channel through which preexisting entities are realized or flow. It is directly relevant to the existence of those entities. Only a strange platonic ontology would permit us to say that a given conference existed as such and only was actualized by using money.

I insist on that point because, interestingly enough, money isn't normally treated that way. In particular, hegemonial, so-called neoclassical economics[3] has always been criticized for conceptualizing money as a neutral tool that only makes preexisting practices of exchange easier to handle (Keen 2011, 14, 243, 298–99; see also Orléan 2014, 14; Kohl 2014, 59–94). We find an explicit statement already in 1848 in John Stuart Mill:

> There cannot, in short, be intrinsically a more insignificant thing, in the economy of society, than money. *It is a machine for doing quickly and commodiously, what would be done, though less quickly and commodiously, without it*: and like many other kinds of machinery, it only exerts a distinct and independent influence of its own when it gets out of order. (Mill 1936, 488; emphasis added)

This statement defines money clearly as a neutral channel that only accelerates and facilitates what exists without it. It stands in radical opposition to our very daily intuitions, namely that money makes the world go round (although interestingly Mill describes money as "machinery"). To refer to just one more example: German economist Wilhelm Gerloff stated in his book *Geld und Gesellschaft* ("Money and Society") from 1952 that in "classical theory" money would be seen only as a "neutral" and "indifferent . . . element" (1952, 217).[4]

This neutralization of money is not only incompatible with a media studies view in the tradition of Kittler. It also has some very dangerous implications, which I can only hint at here: In the aftermath of the so-called financial crisis of 2008, the question frequently came up regarding *who* was to be held accountable. That money rules the world was accepted, albeit always with the additional question: *and who rules money*? If money is seen as a neutral tool or channel, such a question is the logical next step. But this question, often verging on conspiracy theory, ignores the basic teaching of media theory that without money (and its scripts and dynamics) there would be no "greedy banksters" who want to accumulate ever more abstract wealth in the first place. The whole idea of potentially unlimited (and therefore somehow unethical) greed is possible only if one accepts the premise of money as an abstract and therefore potentially infinitely accumulatable medium.

Accumulating an infinite amount of, let's say, apples is impossible, simply because they will rot. Moreover, the idea of people exerting their power through money was historically, especially in the German context, an anti-Semitic cliché. Ultimately, the argument was that money is neutral, but is *misused* by Jewish high finance for their more or less sinister goals—this was a central ideological element of National Socialism. The difference between *schaffendes* (productive) and *raffendes* (parasitic) capital, unfortunately still sometimes implicit in contemporary discourse,[5] *is directly related to the idea that money is a transparent and neutral channel*—it can be put to good or bad ends and transmits these indifferently. Therefore, media studies can and should contribute to this field of problems by providing a description of the specific agency of money, its scripts and limitations. But this is a complicated task for several reasons—as we will see.

In the second section of this chapter I want to sketch out some ideas concerning a possible media-theoretical description of money. Some of the relevant theoretical sources are discussed. One result of this discussion is that actor-network theory (ANT) might be an interesting candidate to work with when describing money as a medium. So in sections three and four I will discuss in more detail the writings of Michel Callon and Bruno Latour on money (and capitalism). I will demonstrate that ANT, at least in its current form, is not really suitable for the task of discussing money as a medium, especially since its reduces money to a transparent channel of pregiven human intentions—contrary to its own claims, firstly to describe human and nonhuman actors *symmetrically,* and secondly to only describe entities that make a difference (*mediators* in contrast to sheer *intermediaries*).[6] In the fifth section, I'll draw a conclusion.

Some General Remarks on Media Theory and Money

What could be the genuine contribution of media studies to the discussion of money, in contrast to the numerous contributions already made by philosophy, sociology, and economics (see, e.g., Ingham 2005)? Shouldn't it be—as already hinted at in the introduction—about the *mediality* of money? The abstract character of money seems to contradict this effort immediately, because no *specific materiality* that might be characteristic for the medium of money, its *mediality*, can be defined easily. Money can exist as metal coins, as paper strips, as numbers stored and transmitted electronically, and in several other forms. So it seems that the aforementioned "neutrality of money" is indeed a fact, insofar as the effects of money do not to depend on any kind of specific mediality.

Perhaps this shows that money is not a medium at all—or at least a medium with a very low specificity.[7] This might also be the reason that theoreticians who are otherwise quite sympathetic to a strong, materiality-centered approach like that of Kittler take—when discussing money—recourse to Luhmannian systems theory and its definition of money as a "symbolically generalized medium of communication" (see Luhmann 1994, 230–71). Ganßmann underlines that the recourse to this definition of money already implies a kind of repression of money's materiality:

> Interestingly enough, all the other "media"—for example, power, confidence, truth, love—simply consist of an invocation of concepts which describe agents' attitudes towards each other or towards norms. Concepts are reified as media by theoretical decision. For money, this seems to work the other way around. Historically, it appears to have started its social role in the form of palpable pieces of precious metal. In a long process of social evolution, symbolic representations were introduced as substitutes for precious metal (coins) in one or the other function of money . . . Thus, money is obviously unique among the media of communication in terms of its history and the direction of its evolution. What, then, is the function of (or the motive for) theoretically treating money on a par with other such media? (Ganßmann 1988, 288)

Norbert Bolz, one of the authors who played an important role in the formation of media studies in Germany in the 1980s, admits right at the beginning of his book *Am Ende der Gutenberg-Galaxis* (1993), which contains a chapter explicitly titled "Geld als Medium" (money as a medium), that a certain eclecticism between Luhmannian systems theory and the (Kittlerian) theory of media is necessary (Bolz 1993, 8). Although this is not directly related to the discussion of money later in the book (Bolz 1993, 90–100), it seems to at least be symptomatic of money not easily being conceptualized with the usual notions of mediality and materiality. For Bolz, following the sociological approach of Luhmann, money is defined by its "code paying / not-paying" (1993, 94) and therefore a "pure medium of computation, freed of all earthly remainders" (1993, 96), meaning of all materiality. Jochen Hörisch wrote in a very similar vein:

> See, new media make everything new. They free us from the dirty aspects characteristic of traditional flows of media—from printing ink, from the eucharistic streams of blood, as well as from the indecent materiality of the pecunia-olet-stream-of-money. The new relations of

> communication are immaterial. Pixels are mostly free of earthly remainders. (Hörisch 2004, 170)[8]

But these and similar arguments for a "transcendental" (Bolz 1993, 95) character of money (that Bolz [2006, 96], following Luhmann, compares to the purely formal status of the Kantian transcendental ego) are problematic at least in two ways: *Firstly,* it remains to be seen if the description of the "medium" of money "as power without characteristics" (Bolz 2006, 94) is really compatible with its specific binary code paying / not-paying. To have *this* code and not another one means that money is at least not "without characteristics."

But *secondly,* more important for my discussion here is the question of whether money can really be described (only) as a "code," as Luhmann and Bolz do, meaning as a medium without materiality, insofar a (binary) code, as it seems, can be implemented in potentially any materiality without changing. Already in Talcott Parsons, who first described money as a symbolically generalized medium of communication, "money is 'essentially a 'symbolic' phenomenon and hence . . . its analysis required a frame of reference closer to that of linguistics than of technology'" (Ganßmann 1988, 290).[9]

Kittler's (1992) provocative thesis that "there is no software"—meaning that the ethereal and immaterial realm of software is erected upon an indispensable material infrastructure (hardware)—might also apply to money. Seitter (2002, 183–86) similarly underlines that it is absurd to speak of the immateriality of money, already given the fact that even money in the form of digital and electronic accounts presupposes an infrastructure of hardware, networks, and so on. Winkler (2004, 39) adds that there is another profoundly material side to money: there is the law, which for example strictly forbids counterfeiting, and the police, who will arrest and detain any counterfeiters behind very material walls.[10]

A traditional banknote is already a highly complex material object, protected against counterfeiting by holographic elements and other elaborate print-document security technologies that can only be realized in high-tech institutions. In this sense, a banknote is not less but even more material than a simple coin made of gold (see Schröter 2015). These materialities are by no means exterior to the operations of money: the much invoked "trust" that is necessary for the functioning of money is based on the (normally implicit) assumption that given banknotes are not counterfeited or—*a fortiori*—given electronic bank accounts are displayed correctly, that my online transactions are secure, and so on. All these operations do not only presuppose a law that forbids counterfeiting and manipulation, and a state that effectively punishes illegal behavior, but *technologies*—"technologies of trust"—that make illegal behavior detectable and traceable in the first place.[11]

Therefore, the materiality, meaning mediality, of given tokens of money is not an "earthly remainder" (as Bolz and Hörisch put it), to be rejected and erased in the near future, but *a very precondition of the operability of money as such.* Here the systematic interrelation between "symbolically generalized media of communication" and media as technologies comes into focus: only when my business partner trusts my money (due to an implicit heterogeneous assemblage of technological, juridical and political actors and operations), the money I offer can enhance the probability that she will accept my offer. This enhancement of the probability of communication is exactly the definition of "symbolically generalized media of communication" (see Luhmann 1994, 253; Ganßmann 1988, 305). Money might be *the* significant case to develop such a perspective, which bridges the gap between hitherto strictly separate definitions of medium.

Obviously, the first, decisive step toward an analysis of money from the perspective of media theory is hereby complete. Although the detailed contours of such a theoretical perspective remain to be developed, some further points can already be raised.

The further elaboration of such a theoretical perspective would not only entail a rereading of the different theoretical discussions of money in media theory (McLuhan, Hörisch, Bolz, Winkler, Rotman, Seitter, Krämer, etc.); it would also be necessary to read classical texts from philosophy, sociology, and, of course, economics for traces and building blocks of a media-theoretical perspective on money. For example: Menger discusses, in his classical text on the "Origins of Money," in which money is explicitly called a "medium of exchange" (1892, 239), the reasons rare metals like gold and silver came to be used as money. Ingham classifies Menger's approach to the field of "orthodox" or "commodity" theories of the genesis of money that describe the emergence of money out of the exchange of commodities: "It is contended that money takes its properties from its status as a commodity with intrinsic (or exchange) value. These are able to act as media of exchange" (Ingham 2005, xi). Metals like silver and gold seem to be "intrinsically" valuable and are therefore chosen or at least chosen by the market: Jones (1976, 775) argues exactly that media of exchange are selected by the market, which leads him to reject alongside "intrinsic value" also those "physical properties" that can be described as aspects of mediality:

> The important point is that this commonness is a market characteristic of goods rather than an intrinsic physical characteristic such as portability, divisibility, or cognizability. This is not to say that such physical characteristics play no role in determining *which* good will be used as a medium of exchange. However the analysis suggests that the rationale for using a medium of exchange in the first place might be found in the differing market characteristics of goods and the decentralized nature of exchange. (1976, 775)

Although he rejects the media-theoretical idea of the importance of the materiality of the medium, he does not seem sure. And of course the most important characteristic—countability, which is no physical but a symbolic property—is not even mentioned. So Jones's argument is at least unclear and has to be confronted with approaches that insist that not markets select media of exchange, as Jones argues, but on the contrary: media of exchange are presuppositions for markets. There have never been markets without such media (Kohl 2014, 280–85). This is close to media theory, insofar as it says that certain media allow practices like markets. And moreover, any concept that argues that money is chosen by the market is vulnerable to, for example, institutional theories that argue that money can only have "value" if the state guarantees it. An institutional-material assemblage seems to be more fundamental than practices of exchange.

Anyway, the discussion between "orthodox" or "metallist" versus "nominalist" or "institutionalist" theories of money is not my central concern here, nor is the alleged "intrinsic value" (that might or might not result from the labor necessary to produce them) of the metals. But Ingham (2005, xiv; see also 132) also states with regard to Menger: "Coinage is explained with the further conjecture that precious metals have additional advantageous, or 'efficient', properties—such as durability, divisibility, portability, etc." This aspect is more interesting here: the materials, e.g. gold and silver, firstly, *cannot easily be produced* by ordinary citizens, meaning: the coins cannot easily be counterfeited—and that's far more important for their operability as the alleged "intrinsic value" of gold and silver. The metals are chosen because they can be cut in precisely defined pieces that can be *counted.* They are *durable* and cannot corrode or burn easily—that is, they can "store" value in a reliable way (soap bubbles are definitely not very practical as a currency).

Their durability also means that they, secondly, are able to carry *nominal values* in the form of inscriptions that cannot be changed easily. The nominal value relates the money-media to a "money of account," which is very central for some approaches to money (see Ingham 2005, xvi–xvii). There have been forms of money that didn't carry a nominal value, but in which the value was directly related to materiality in the sense that, for example, such and such a quantity of gold was correlated to such and such a value (in a sense, such money is partially an analog medium). But, firstly, this kind of money is obviously prone to corrosion, insofar as any loss (unintended or intended) of the quantity of gold per coin reduces value (see Caffentzis [1989, 17–44] on clipped coins; see Rotman [1987, 22–26] for the argument that this at least caused the emergence of nominal values). Secondly, the relation of such and such a quantity of gold to such and such a nominal value remains of course conventional and is in that sense still not "intrinsic."

Whatever else money may be, it is a medium that makes it possible to attach countable numbers ("prices") to concrete objects or processes, in what may be described as the role of money in the operation of "measuring" value (see Ingham 2005; Engster 2014). Because of its structural countability, the code of money is digital, as Seitter (2002, 181) argues.[12] The "convergence between the logic of mathematical disciplines . . . and the logic of the mode of production," as Alexander Galloway (2013) puts it in his recent critique of speculative realism, is therefore not just a contemporary phenomenon "during the period of digital capitalism" (2013, 359), as he himself acknowledges in a footnote. The "mathematization of production" (359) is implicit in capitalism from its very beginning, insofar as value (however it is derived) is expressed, measured, and accumulated in the abstract form of exchange value, which finally finds its embodiment in digital, countable, and therefore mathematically describable money (and even the most complex "derivates" traded at stock markets today stem from this basic mathematical logic of money). Capitalism is from its very beginning the formalization and digitization of economy, even of society as a whole.

To sum up: The digital code of money needs media that have a certain durability, countability, anticounterfeitability and thus trustworthiness (that is the site where materiality is entangled with the law and the state), and these properties make certain media interesting as money (rather than their status as "precious metals"—quite the contrary: their preciousness is the effect of those properties). Money is pure countability, operationalized in suitable media and *therefore it is counted.* This last statement is not as trivial as it sounds: the point is that the usage of a medium that is only countable leads to the counting of everything and to the description of everything in the categories of "less" and "more" where more is equated with "better." *The countable, digital specificity of money leads (at least potentially) to the phenomenon of accumulation.* This fundamental media logic of money is something that is repressed in ANT, as we will see below.

But although these quite basic characteristics are irreducible for the operations of money, that doesn't mean, obviously, that the media of money have never changed. Besides the media *theory* of money, which was very sketchily hinted at above, there is also a media *history* of money. And the change of the media of money is far more complex and interesting than the often repeated reductionist teleological trajectory toward ever increasing "immateriality," in which—as is sometimes suggested[13]—the medium of money reveals its proper essence as digital code. This Hegelian figure is questionable for several reasons. Firstly, it is not clear why money should unfold in this way at all; it might simply transform through a series of historically contingent configurations, in which, beside some basic properties that remain stable (otherwise different historical phenomena could not even be compared as *different forms* of money), other features radically change due to religious, political, social, cultural, or even intermedial reasons—and may also change back.[14] Secondly, the basic narrative seems flawed: is the production of gold coins or paper strips with an imprinted nominal value really more "material" than the vast and global network and computer infrastructure necessary for electronic banking today? Isn't it the other way round?

I will mention just one example that is quite interesting in this regard: Micronesian stone money (Gillilland 1975). This example might at first seem to be confirming the narrative of immaterialization, but stone money has been used for a long time alongside newer currencies.

One could debate if this is money at all (see Kohl 2014, 83–87), but at least it is also digital (it can be counted), it is (very) durable, it

[Figure 1.] Stone Money. Source: https://commons.wikimedia.org/wiki/File:Yap_Stone_Money.jpg. Photograph by Eric Guinther, copyright CC BY-SA 3.0.

cannot easily be counterfeited, and it is trusted. But it has at least one crucial difference to what we call money today. Due to its sheer size and materiality, it cannot be accumulated, you cannot pile up an infinite amount as you can, at least in principle, with the (in this sense it is true) more dematerialized electronic units of currency we have today. So one aspect of the money, namely its potential to be accumulated (and to be circulated easily), is not given (and it cannot be transported easily, so transportability might not be a necessary feature of money). Jappe (2005, 166) even argues that such forms of money with an excessive materiality (he uses the example of Spartanian metal bars) were invented to block the possibilities of accumulation *intentionally,* because the drive to accumulate was seen as disruptive for communal life. This seems to be consistent with the historical studies by Jacques LeGoff (2012) and others (e.g., Kurz 2012, 68–134), which note that the existence of money as such is not identical with the existence of capitalism—solely when the accumulation of ever *more* money becomes the *central principle* of society, then we can speak of capitalism, but I cannot go into that discussion here more deeply. At least this discussion suggests that there might be noncapitalist money. Or perhaps the stuff called "money" in precapitalist societies isn't money in the modern sense or even money at all.

That points to a final and complicated problem for a media theory—namely the relation of the medium of money to society. Does the medium determine society (as in the classic Kittlerian position)? That markets presuppose money seems a case in point. Or is it the other way around, insofar there is no trustworthy money without the law and the state? Does the usage of money finally and unavoidably result in capitalism, that is, a society completely centered around the reproduction of the medium—which comes close to teleological models of the historical unfolding of the medium? On the one hand, the seemingly progressive acceleration of the circulation of money (nowadays by transforming money into electronic signals) seems to be the *necessary precondition* for this drive to accumulate. On the other hand, this ever increasing and accelerating speed of circulation might be the *result* of the drive to accumulate.[15]

But perhaps the questions are posed wrongly; perhaps this complicated problem (which at least is the problem of the emergence of capitalism as such) is better described as a kind of *co-constitution* of money and capital (capital defined as the ongoing and accelerating process of making more money out of money). So it seems advisable that the further development of a media theory of money tries to avoid the sterile discussion on determinism. That's why it might seem promising to use ANT as an approach to analyze the medium of money, because ANT's promise is to avoid distinctions such as "technology" (or "medium") versus "society" in the first place. As Latour (2005, 75–76) writes: "There exists no relation whatsoever between 'the material' and 'the social world,' because it is this very division which is a complete artifact . . . There is no empirical case where the existence of two coherent and homogeneous aggregates, for instance technology 'and' society, could make any sense."

In the following two sections I will read texts of Michel Callon and Bruno Latour, main protagonists of ANT, closely and will discuss their theories of money and capitalism. Both authors explicitly addressed that topic, Callon even published a volume entitled *The Laws of the Markets* in 1998 and has since been one of the main protagonists of the so-called "performativity of economics" debate.[16] But my readings will try to show that both authors miss (due to a certain "praxeological" bias of ANT) the logic of money (and the logic of capitalism). That shows that the development of a media theory of money cannot make use of ANT, or at least should use the heuristic principles of ANT in a modified way. It may be disappointing that the present article doesn't develop the promised theory in detail but instead focuses on the critique of other approaches. But that's a necessary beginning to define one's own position—I will come back to this in the conclusion.

The Repression of Money in ANT I: Michel Callon

Capitalism/Kapitalism

Callon writes:

> I use the word Kapitalism, with a capital K, to denote the reality imagined by everyone who considers the Western economic system to be a homogeneous reality, endowed *with its own logic*. The assumption of a homogeneous economic reality is made by those who criticize capitalism,[17] thus defined, as well as by those who defend it by talking of the market and its laws, in general. Experiments[18] in past decades have shown that Kapitalism could only be a fiction: no program has managed to make Kapitalism exist nor to overthrow it. There are only capitalisms. (Callon 2007, 354; emphasis added)

A typical move for praxeocentric discourses (i.e. discourses implicitly or explicitly privileging human practice) is to deny the possibility of an "inherent logic" in relation to nonhuman entities—the argument is always that entities are situated in historical and local practices and therefore are always different without any underlying homogeneous logic (see Callon 2005, 15: "I don't believe in A Kapitalism that could be reduced to AN impersonal logic."). Firstly, it is simply not true that the critics of capitalism, at whom Callon's argument is obviously directed (which is presumably why he uses the German-sounding "Kapitalism" to allude to the Marxist tradition), postulate a homogeneous entity called "capitalism." "They" always admitted that capitalism has had historical phases named, for example, "imperialism" and "state-monopolistic capitalism" or, in another theoretical vein, "Fordism" and "post-Fordism," or that there is "uneven development," etc. They just postulated that capitalism has one or more fundamental principles that remain in place below historical and local differences (as is the case when we speak of the media logic of money); that is why Marx analyzes capitalism in "its ideal average" (Marx 1991, 970; see Hodgson 2016).

Secondly and far more importantly, Callon unwittingly admits that, too: how could he even speak of "different capitalisms"? He presupposes a fundamental principle common to all these capitalisms or otherwise he couldn't even classify the different phenomena under the same label. Consider this symptomatic quote by Callon:

> Instead of assuming, for example, the existence of a spirit of capitalism or an overall logic of a mode of production, we can relate certain forms of economic activity to the more or less chaotic, regular, and general upsurge of calculative agencies formatted and equipped to act on the basis of a logic of accumulation and maximization. (Callon 2005, 5)

At first the idea of an "overall logic of a mode of production" is negated—but then self-contradictorily "a logic of accumulation and maximization" (that is of course the logic of capitalist accumulation) is reintroduced.

This typical praxeocentric fallacy is repeated over and over in his texts, and it finds its most radical expression in a statement he quotes approvingly: "Rationality is always situated" (Callon 1998b, 48). Clearly, this is not even a false statement—it is as nonsensical as the statement "there is no truth," because it contradicts itself: it states as universally true, that is as nonsituated, that every truth is situated. For Callon, it seems to be universally rational to assume that rationality is never universal but always situated—that is self-contradictory. A radical praxeocentrism dissolving everything into locally and historically situated occurrences is *logically impossible*: it could not even compare two different occurrences to highlight their local specificity, because to compare them, a general principle of comparison (e.g. that both occurrences are "practices") already has to be taken into account.

One of the main goals of Callon's whole approach, and one I find quite appealing, is to show that markets are nothing natural and that the calculative agencies required in markets have to be constructed. Although Callon (1998b, 6) rejects "sociocultural frames," he mentions such things as the law and the state, which also were named as preconditions for markets in the Marxian tradition (see Pashukanis 2002). But he insists particularly on the way in which *homo economicus* is produced. While the *homo economicus* would in the Marxian tradition perhaps be subsumed under the admittedly problematic notion of "ideology," Callon is more interested in the concrete tools and operations that produce "calculativeness" on the side of the human actors and "calculability" on the side of the objects. Immediately, the question arises, *what* is calculated and *why* there is calculation at all? "Competition between calculative agencies . . . is largely determined by the respective qualities of the calculating devices. The probability of gain is on the side of the agency with the greatest power of calculation . . ." (Callon 1998b, 45).

Competition and the goal of "gain" are presupposed here and explain why calculation is used. This implies that Callon presupposes a social form in which any entity besides their specific and unique use-value has also an *abstract exchange value,* because only such an abstract value can be calculated. Without using these Marxian notions, he admits this in one of his examples (see Callon 2007, 336–39), Norwegian fishers that are turned into economic subjects by transforming the fish into calculable "cyborg-fish"; that is, commodities. This is nothing else than a reinvention of what Marx (1990, 873–907) called "primitive accumulation," in which objects are violently transformed into objects that have exchange value (and besides may be useful).[19] For Marx, primitive accumulation is the precondition of the establishment of capitalist societies. But Callon does not use the term "value" systematically in *The Laws of the Markets.* Sometimes he speaks of "usage value" (1998b, 33) or "use value" (35), "exchange value" is only to be found in a quote (19), so that basically it remains unclear *what* exactly is calculated in Callon's approach.[20]

Calculation and Money

At this precise point we have to return to the question of a "specific logic." Shouldn't we say that the reduction of everything to exchangeable, calculable abstract quantities—a process that is also implied in Callon's central notion of "framing" (see below)—is *specific* to capitalism? This is at least the answer Marxian theory would give: capitalism is most generally to be understood as the total reign of the abstract value-form, represented in money, meaning that everything, especially labor-power, is turned into exchangeable commodities with an exchange value that is measured or at least represented in its price (see Larsen et al. 2014). Due to his praxeocentrism, we should expect that Callon denies this, especially since it would force him to accept the existence of Kapitalism (with a capital "K"); and this is indeed the case:

> There is no Great Divide between societies populated by calculative agencies and societies in which the agents do not calculate. Even Deleuze and Guattari were on the wrong track with their concept of deterritorialization, that extraordinary faculty bestowed on capitalism for breaking

> all ties and undoing solidarity . . . So-called traditional societies are populated—sometimes even over-populated with calculative agencies. (Callon 1998b, 39)

Callon argues that there is *no* "great" divide between societies with and without calculative agencies, because there are no societies that do not calculate: there was always calculation, and as a consequence there is nothing special about capitalism; no Kapitalism exists. In consequence, we would either have to abandon the term "capitalism" or we would have to call all societies, even "so-called traditional societies," capitalist, acknowledging that there are indeed only different capitalisms and no Kapitalism with any underlying specific principle. But this argument leads Callon to argue against himself: by stretching the principle of calculation to all societies and thereby erasing any (small or great) "divide," he is the one who homogenizes unduly.

It is difficult to understand why he rejects, on the one hand, a homogenizing principle ("Kapitalism") that allow us to relate different "capitalisms" to each other and, on the other hand, introduces an even wider homogenizing principle—calculation as such—that surprisingly and ahistorically unites "traditional societies" (by which, I guess, he means so-called primitive societies) and modern industrial capitalism under one category. His argumentation, however, is not only logically unconvincing but also historically wrong. If we assume that Callon relates the question of calculation to the existence of money (because he talks about the economy and not about mathematics), he would have to argue (if calculation is his homogenizing principle) that the sheer existence of money already means that there is capitalism. But that's wrong. As already mentioned, as Jacques Le Goff (2012) and others have shown, even the existence of money (as a materialization of calculation) does not make a society capitalist. Money is much older than capitalism.

The question is if a society is *centered* around money and its scripts (to use a term from Akrich's 1992 essay). Only when the basic script is M-C-M′, meaning that money (M) is used to produce commodities

(C) that are sold for more money (M), and when this script is fundamental for all activities—only then we can speak of capitalism (see, for a recent and particularly pointed argument, Lotz 2014). At least this is a definition that avoids the confusion created by Callon. This script (M-C-M′) is the definition of capital, according to Marx (1990, 247–57): capital is the *process* of making more money out of money. Marx (1990, 166–67) writes: "They do this without being aware of it." Marx's definition implies that there is a script to money regulating our practices. Money is not just a transparent means for human ends existing independently of money as a praxeocentric theory would have it—and as neoclassical economics as a form of praxeocentrism[21] puts it, in which money plays nearly no role (see, among a lot of other authors, Pahl 2008, 9–16).

Money is, as media theorists like Sybille Krämer (2005, 88–89) underline, *the* medium of calculability. It is pure quantity and therefore its quantum can only diminish or grow. It is not surprising that in its practical use its quantum diminishes or grows. It is also not surprising that economic actors "calculate," as Callon rightly insists, because money can *only* be calculated with. All markets should be (and practically are) centered around calculability. But Callon always insists in a typically praxeocentric manner that there are only *different* markets: "The idea of the market as a unified category and institution is progressively disappearing" (Callon, in Barry and Slater 2002, 291). Yet surely no one would trade and calculate on markets if the outcome wasn't *more money* than the amount invested.

Callon (1998b, 12) states: "The agent is calculative because action can only be calculative." Firstly, this statement fails to differentiate economic practice ("action") from every other practice and thereby again underlines the status of calculation as Callon's homogenizing principle. Secondly, Callon deduces calculativeness from *action* ("because action can only be calculative"), that is, from practice and not from the central role of a medium whose script is pure calculability. Although the role of devices, technologies, and so on is so central for Callon's argument, they are (at least sometimes) reduced to useful tools in the hands of human actors. This is especially (and very significantly) the case for money. It seems that Callon, implicitly following the economic mainstream, also follows the neoclassical mainstream's exclusion and oblivion of money.[22] In Callon's discourse the script of money tends to disappear, and although Callon implies, as I have cited above, the goal of "gain" as central for markets (Callon 1998b, 45), the explicit "imperative of profitability is absent" (Fine 2003, 480). We can expect that this discursive operation appears as a reduction and erasure of the pure quantitativeness, calculability, and abstraction of money: that is, its mediality. That is exactly the case.

Money, Commodity, Production

Callon begins with describing the specific medial form of money:

> To be sure its main contribution was to provide a unit of account without which no calculation would be possible. However the essential is elsewhere. Money is required above all—even if this point is often overlooked—to delimit the circle of actions between which equivalence can be formulated. It makes commensurable that which was not so before . . . It provides the currency, the standard, the common language which enables us to reduce heterogeneity, to construct an equivalence and to create a translation . . . It is the final piece, the keystone in a metrological system that is already in place and of which it merely guarantees the unity and coherence. *Alone it can do nothing*; combined with all the measurements preceding it, it facilitates a calculation which makes commensurable that which was not so before. (Callon 1998b, 21–22; emphasis added)

At first sight, he seems to acknowledge the script of money—but with a significant twist: money is added as the endpoint of a metrological chain of measurements operating in a world without money. There is a world performatively produced as calculable by measurement and then money comes in—"merely" as a "final piece." "Alone it can do nothing"—meaning it is reduced to an intermediary, that is an entity that "transports meaning or force without transformation" (Latour 2005, 39). But again he doesn't explain how "equivalence" is achieved, how money is related to "measurement": that is, *what it measures.* Yet some theory of value would be needed, which Callon does not provide.

But to reduce money to the "final piece" also negates that in the world we live in everything is already produced with regard to money. Nothing is produced that doesn't at least potentially yield more money than was invested—and this rule even shapes the commodities in a very concrete way: think of so-called planned obsolescence (see Bulow 1986). In Callon's model[23] money is added as a market device to a production devoid of money—even more so: production does not appear. To be sure, "producers" are mentioned a lot (Callon 1998b, 18, 19, 20, and passim), but there is no description or theory of production. But if production is already structured with regard to money, money is not just a practical means of exchange. Commodities are things that have a price; that is, they are equivalent to some amount of money. Being a commodity means being a thing *and* being money.

Callon (1999, 189) writes about the being of a commodity: "to transform something into a commodity, it is necessary to cut the ties between this thing and other objects or human beings one by one." The central notion here is "framing":

> a clear and precise boundary must be drawn between the relations which the agents will take into account and which will serve in their calculations, on the one hand, and the multitude of relations which will be ignored by the calculation as such, on the other. (1999, 186–87; see also Callon 1998c)

The objects simply seem to be there, out of nothing, and framing seems to mean ripping them out of, for example, emotional contexts to sell them. This looks more like a flea market than a real economy in which commodities *are produced as commodities for the markets*. Callon (1999, 189) writes: "one is not born a commodity, one becomes it." This is simply wrong for the vast majority of objects surrounding us.

Although the book is called *The Laws of the Markets,* Callon speaks right on the first page of the introduction of "economy" (1998b, 1), as if markets and (capitalist) economy were identical. He only talks about markets. This is also typical for the neoclassical approach, which tends to focus on exchange (see, for example, Orléan 2014, 37). To argue that way is to erase production, which means to erase capital from the picture, understood as M-C-M'. Capital in this sense means that the production of commodities is part of the movement of value, where commodities and money are in a way the same, namely metamorphoses of capital (see Marx 1990, 255). It seems that Callon has this theoretical (Marxian) argument in mind when he writes:

> Money seems to be the epitome of the commodity; it is pure equivalence, pure disentanglement, pure circulation. Yet, as Viviana Zelizer showed so convincingly, agents are capable of constantly creating private money which embodies and conveys ties . . . This is the case of grandmothers who gives her grand-daughter silver coins, or supermarkets which give fidelity vouchers to their customers. (Callon 1999, 190)

It is strange that Callon defines the commodity by framing, that is untying ("cut the ties between this thing and other objects or human beings one by one" [1999, 189])—but at the same time doubts that money is "disentanglement" and follows Zelizer (1998) on "money which embodies and conveys ties." With this argument, he again separates commodities from money (because only commodities seem to follow the basic operation of "framing"), although commodities can only be understood *as* commodities in relation to money. Giving away a thing on the market (and in that sense "untying" it from me as the seller) means exchanging it against money—money is the force that allows generalized "untying" and in that sense it is "pure disentanglement." It is a basic move in Callon to tear apart money and the commodity—to erase the basic logic of capitalism.

Or see a similar quote from a different publication:

> Earmarking is deployed as much in the domestic sphere, with silver coins which a grandmother gifts to her grand-children to put in their piggybanks in memory of her, as in systems of mass distribution, with vouchers, fidelity or credit cards and other such devices. (Callon 1998b, 35)

This is highly symptomatic: the coins grandma gives her grand-daughter are treated as "private money," that is a form of money proper, although these coins cannot be exchanged against com-modities. Grandma can give as many coins as she wants to her granddaughter, she could even produce new "private money" by writing the word *money* on paper snippets as much as she likes, but she shouldn't try to go to a supermarket (even to one that emits vouchers) and try to acquire commodities with the private money.[24] "Private money" is not money at all.

Armin Beverungen made an important comment on an earlier version of this text. He problematized the formulation "private money is not money at all," by invoking as an example M-Pesa, a very successful digital currency issued by Vodafone and Safaricom, first realized in Kenya in 2007. He seemed to understand my argument as directed against all currencies that are emitted by *privately owned companies,* although I made it only in relation to Callon's example, which isn't about a privately owned company but about "silver coins which a grandmother gifts to her grandchildren" (Callon 1998b, 35). Money emitted by private companies can be money in the full sense, as the case of M-Pesa shows (my sources are Hughes and Lonie 2007; Makin 2011; Wölbert 2015). Firstly, the whole development was subsidized by a public-sector challenge grant, meaning that M-Pesa is not a child of private enterprises alone. But secondly, and far more importantly, it was developed in close conversation with regulating bodies and the Kenyan government concerning questions of security, customer identity, trustworthiness, and so on. The forms of state currency are, at least partially, mapped onto the digital currency, otherwise it wouldn't work. In that sense, it remains deeply connected to the law and the state. Thirdly, it is therefore not an alternative to the official state currency: costumers go to an agent, where they can deposit or withdraw cash from their e-money accounts. That means that M-Pesa is convertible into official state currency and vice versa. It is just a different form of distribution for state currency.

None of the three points apply to "silver coins which a grandmother gifts to her grandchildren." Callon's example is from the—as he writes—"domestic sphere" and therefore really *private*. And this type of private money is not money at all, whereas M-Pesa, deeply anchored in state currency, law, the state, and so on, is money. We should avoid confusing the two meanings of "private," on the one hand the "private" (in the sense of "domestic") sphere and on the other hand "privately owned" companies (in contrast to, let's say, state departments). Tokens circulating in the "private sphere" are not money. Seitter (2002, 188; my translation) writes: "What Wittgenstein said of language, although he spoke of 'language games,' is true for money too: there is no private language." *Human actors can of course name anything "money," but that doesn't turn it into money—which demonstrates that there's an irreducible script that cannot be easily changed by different practices.*

Callon (1998b, 35, 54) gives an example of a prostitute who writes the day and the date of an especially beautiful night with a client on a banknote—this is an example that "the banknote is an excellent medium for the exercise of rewriting." Apart from the interesting point that he explicitly calls the banknote a medium, he wants to argue that money is not abstract and that its "official attachments" can be "overloaded" with "new, private, messages" (1998b, 35). What does he want so say? Of course, I can use a banknote as medium of writing, but if he wants to suggest that the role of money is thereby changed from the universal equivalent, pure calculability, to something personal and individual (as the individual banknote might be) this is simply outlandish. In a similar way, you could say that you can change the rules of soccer by writing some personal notes on the ball. Money is again severed from the notion of commodity. *The script of money is repressed in favor of practices by human actors. ANT's own principle of symmetry is violated.* Remember Latour's (2005, 76) formulation: "To be symmetric, for us, simply means *not* to impose a priori some spurious *asymmetry* among human intentional action and a material world of causal relations." But Callon exactly establishes such an asymmetry.

The Repression of Money in ANT II: Bruno Latour

One can find a similar repression of money in the work of Bruno Latour, which suggests that this repression might be characteristic for the whole discourse of ANT. Latour writes, discussing capitalism in a way similar to Callon:

> Once its ordinary character is recognized, the "abstraction" of money can no longer be the object of a fetish cult . . . "Capitalism" is . . . an empty word as long as precise material instruments are not proposed to explain any capitalization at all, be it of specimens, books, information or money. (Latour 1986, 31)

Hence, Latour criticizes the description of money as a fetish based on the abstraction of value (central to modern sociality in a Marxian perspective). Although this complex topic cannot be discussed here in detail, Latour is of course alluding to Marx's notion of the fetish (see Marx 1990, 163–77).[25] Somewhat similar to Callon, Latour argues against the Marxian tradition. Money, according to Latour, is "ordinary" because it resembles other *immutable mobiles*. What does this term mean? It refers to all processes that transmit specific information that remains stable during this process of transmission. Latour mentions "printing, linear perspective, geometric projections and transformations collectively, cartographic discoveries, the camera obscura; and also processes for accounting and for producing graphs, tables and statistics of all kinds" (Schüttpelz 2009, 70). These processes enable the accumulation of knowledge in what Latour calls *centers of calculation,* that is, military high commands, government authorities, and scientific and bureaucratic centers of power. This accumulation of knowledge allows to rule the entities about which knowledge has been accumulated. Hence, Latour (1986, 13) writes on the role of the immutable mobiles in the history of "the West": "*Anything* that will accelerate the mobility of the traces that a location may obtain about another place, or *anything* that will allow these traces to move without transformation from one place to another, will be favored." Schüttpelz (2009, 70; emphasis added) explains:

> Every increase in mobility and every increase in immutability through transformations can help organizations to regulate the distances in a space and obtain small organizational advantages in an *agonistic* relation to other organizations.

Latour's demand for "precise material instruments" means that the fetish remains an all-too-nebulous description; by way of contrast, immutable mobiles (in Latour's view) make it possible to explain the dynamism of capitalism as a process of "capitalization." Instead of saying "capital is the movement of the valorisation of value" (as Marxians would have it), the question would be: "how is this accumulation (capitalization) of money realized in detailed terms?"[26] Money is one immutable mobile among others in this regard. Returning to Latour:

> As soon as money starts to circulate through different cultures, it develops a few clear-cut characteristics: it is mobile (once in small pieces), it is immutable (once in metal), it is countable (once it is coined), combinable, and can circulate from the things valued to the center that evaluates and back . . . As a type of immutable mobile

> *amongst others* it has, however, received too little attention . . . Money is neither more nor less "material" than map making, engineering drawings or statistics. (Latour 1986, 30–31)

Obviously, Latour agrees in principle with the media-theoretical descriptions of money given in section one of this chapter. But the following two key questions arise from this outline of Latour's argument:

(a) Symmetry of the immutable mobiles? Categorizing money amongst other equally ranked immutable mobiles could be problematic—in two ways: it could, first, be that the relation of money to other immutable mobiles is asymmetric and, second, following on from the first point, Latour's argument could be problematic because it ignores the centrality of money at least in capitalist societies. Schüttpelz writes:

> Latour's observation brings the continuity of scientific practice into focus, as well as the unceasing, time- and capital-intensive maintenance of symbolic stability . . . The actual establishment and heightening of the combined properties of "mobility" and "immutability" are based on conditions that are neglected in many media histories, especially a significant increase in capital expenditure for transport infrastructure and education as well as for state and commercial research investment since the late 18th century. It was only with this investment that cartographic recording of European and non-European territories was stabilized and unified; and this investment did indeed lead to the far more consistent text reproduction of 19th-century printing . . . Media innovation, technical standardization and laboratory culture were first united in the laboratory of the 19th century, and this already presupposed a whole host of capital- and time-intensive developments. (Schüttpelz 2013, 36)

In this account, it is noteworthy that the properties of the immutable mobiles—mobility and immutability—are *conditioned* above all by "capital expenditure" and "investment." Clearly, money and its accumulation *are the condition of possibility for other immutable mobiles*—and indeed, the complex machinery and media of recording and dissemination all cost money for development, procurement, and utilization. But then money is precisely not *one immutable mobile among others* but their *conditio sine qua non.*[27] All media (at least in capitalism) presuppose money for their technological infrastructure, their skilled workers, the production of their content. This is a first indication of a fundamental asymmetry. There are other such indications.

Latour (2005, 30) himself emphasizes, as one of the key methodological premises of ANT, that "actors, too, have their own elaborate and fully reflexive meta-language." Unlike "critical sociology," Latour does not wish to "render actors mute altogether": "Are the concepts of the actors allowed to be stronger than that of the analysts, or is it the analyst who is doing all the talking?" (2005, 30). How can this premise be combined with the presupposed ordinariness of money—in view of the phenomenon that sentences like "Money rules the world" or "Money makes the world go round" are part of everyday language, that there is a vast literature of money management guides and that the Cree proverb (Daley 2009, 89) warning that you cannot eat money once adorned every "alternative" cafe? Are there not "concepts of actors" that acknowledge that money is not just an arbitrary immutable mobile among others? Should this not be taken seriously?

Finally, Latour's account contains a peculiar feature that once again indicates an asymmetry. As cited above, he says that money—just like the other immutable mobiles[28]—can "circulate from the things valued to the center that evaluates and back." What does this mean? A central authority that evaluates things is precisely what is lacking under market allocation—unlike, say, the central price-setting in Stalinist planned economies. Moreover, even where centralized planning authorities exist, the setting of prices does not proceed by means of money circulating to the center so that things can *then* be evaluated. Or does Latour's formulation refer to the fact that central banks can vary the quantity of money and hence at least indirectly alter the value of things, inasmuch as an (excessive) increase in the quantity of money would lead to, for example, inflation and hence price rises (at least according to monetarist theory)? But even if one were to accept this, it would not really correspond to the description according to which money can "circulate from the things valued to the center that evaluates and back." Latour may be imposing onto money a scheme that works for other immutable mobiles, even though it does not quite fit here. And this strange reference to a "center that evaluates" suggests something else: Latour takes many other examples of immutable mobiles from the spheres of the military (see also Law 1987), state bureaucracies, or the sciences.[29] These examples concern technologies that are, in part, highly developed and only usable by specialists. By contrast, everyone has to use money. Again, there appears to be an asymmetry here.

(b) What means ". . . will be favored"? Let us recall the crucial sentence from Latour (1986, 13): "*Anything* that will accelerate the mobility of the traces that a location may obtain about another place, or *anything* that will allow these traces to move without transformation from one place to another, will be favored." "Will be favored"—why? And by whom? Latour (1986, 14) writes: "It is, first of all, the unique advantage they give in the rhetorical or polemical situation. 'You doubt of what I say? I'll show you.'" The point is to assert one's own position: immutable mobiles are allies in this enterprise, displaying evidence that is hard to ignore. As Schüttpelz (2009, 70) clarifies, organizations can "obtain small organizational advantages in an agonistic relation to other organizations" if they increase mobility and "immutability across transformations." Hence, it is a matter of *agon* and *polemos,* of competition and even war. In both these areas, immutable mobiles are allies. To once again quote Latour at length:

> Who will win in an agonistic encounter between two authors, and between them and all the others they need to build up a statement? Answer: *the one able to muster on the spot the largest number of well aligned and faithful allies.* This definition of victory is common to war, politics, law, and, I shall now show, to science and technology. My contention is that writing and imaging cannot by themselves explain the changes in our scientific societies, except insofar as *they help to make this agonistic situation more favorable* . . . If we remain at the level of the visual aspects only, we fall back into a series of weak clichés or are led into all sorts of fascinating problems of scholarship far away from our problem; but, on the other hand, if we concentrate on the agonistic situation alone, the principle of any victory, any solidity in science and technology escapes us forever. We have to hold the two eyepieces together so that we turn it into a real *binocular*. (Latour 1986, 5)

It is becoming clear that the "agonistic situation" is being presupposed—initially, it would appear, as equiprimordial with the "level of the visual aspects,"[30] that is the immutable mobiles. But it is more: it is a "reference point" (1986, 13); it is the driving force behind the use of immutable mobiles that are increasingly mobile and increasingly immutable. To quote Latour (1986, 18) again: "This trend toward simpler and simpler inscriptions that mobilize larger and larger numbers of events in one spot, cannot be understood if separated from the agonistic model that we use as our point of reference." The "agonistic model" is thus posited in order to explain the genesis of immutable mobiles—and not *vice versa.* It is already there.

What exactly the various organizations are that stand in an agonistic relation is made clear in a passage in Schüttpelz (2009, 106): "Standardization always occurs agonistically: in competition with other companies (or state authorities) and with the intention of commercial (or bureaucratic) expansion." Can it not be said that a certain commercial and thus market-economic model of "perfect competition," as it is called in neoclassical economics (see Keen 2011, 74–102), provides the template for Callon's agonistic model? And doesn't that remind us of the positions that the media suitable as money are selected by the market—thereby privileging the practice of exchange over the medium, even though historical studies have shown that markets are the effect of money and not its precondition?

And finally: Does this not fundamentally contradict Latour's own elaborate efforts in the entire first part of his *Reassembling the Social* to distinguish ANT from conventional sociologies precisely inasmuch as for ANT "there is *no* preferable type of social aggregates" (Latour 2005, 40)? Instead of presupposing what the ingredients of the social are, ANT aims to observe how actors form bonds with each other. But how, then, can it assume an apparently universal "agonistic model," especially when ANT "maintains there is nothing that is purely universal" (Koch 2009, 6)? How, for instance, can it reject the a priori conviction that "society is unequal and hierarchical" (Latour 2005, 64) from the outset but accept that it is agonistic and polemical (instead of, say, cooperative, what doubtlessly can also be observed[31]) from the outset? How can one of its "basic hypotheses" consist in "the refusal to give an a priori definition of the actor" (Callon 1999, 182)[32] and yet its actors nonetheless be defined as a priori antagonistic? There seems to be a certain conflict between the methodological premises of ANT and a certain ideological subtext in Latour.

This observation can be confirmed by critically discussing the idea of "description" central to ANT: Latour insists that the task of ANT is pure and neutral description: "I told you, we are in the business of descriptions" (2005, 146). But a "pure description" without any premises is impossible; even if it were possible, it is never completed, because networks are infinite; and even if it were possible and it could be completed in a meaningful way, the question still remains what exactly the use is in simply doubling and mirroring an existing practice (and/or network). Purely doubling the practices of actors makes social science superfluous—Callon, by the way, admits that: after having written "that social scientists don't have special access to a truth that would be inaccessible to actors themselves," some lines later he states:

> The role of the anthropology of (the) econom(y)ics *[sic]* is, I believe, to make these anthropological struggles explainable in their theoretical and practical dimensions, by *identifying and revealing the forces* that, in a more or less articulated way, challenge the dominant models and their grip on real markets. (Callon 2005, 12; emphasis added)

Here, the social scientist or anthropologist "reveals" and "identifies" something, meaning that it obviously has been hidden and misunderstood before, hidden to the actors involved and misunderstood by them. Obviously, scientists also according to Callon need access "to a truth that would be inaccessible to actors themselves"—otherwise they simply would be no scientists and couldn't "explain" anything, a notion Callon uses in the quote. The intended pure description is not possible. Description is always already affected by background models. The conclusion seems unavoidable that the "agonistic model" is precisely one such ideological and political model structuring the discourse of ANT—or at least ANT as performed by Callon and Latour.

That would only be permissible if this model were proclaimed to be the "natural" and hence only possible form—but this would contradict not only the premises of ANT[33] but also historical observations to the effect that societies have by no means always been organized in a market form and indeed that a "disembedding" of markets (from religious and guild structures) was required to make them into a central mediating entity in modern societies (see Polanyi 2002).

One conclusion that emerges from points (a) and (b) is that the rejection of the "fetish cult" in favor of "precise material instruments" in order to explain capitalization has two problems. First, the "precise material instruments" appear to presuppose money as their condition of possibility, which means that money cannot be symmetrically categorized among the other immutable mobiles. Money determines the situation of the immutable mobiles too. And, second, the development and distribution of the immutable mobiles apparently depends on an "agonistic model"—the market—that in the context of Latour's argument appears to be ahistorical[34] and possibly even an anthropological norm, whereas critical approaches, such as neo-Marxian theory, conversely attempt to describe and explain the historical establishment of this (or other) model(s).

Instead of being one immutable mobile among others, money seems to be—as my reading of Latour tries to show—*their model.* But this knowledge of the centrality of money and how Latour in his theoretical practice follows the scripts of the medium (and thereby contradicts his manifest praxeocentrism) is repressed.

It is interesting that there is a kind of mirror symmetry between Callon and Latour on money. Callon upholds an a priori asymmetry between human actors and money, reducing the latter to a tool and neutral channel, to an intermediary (in the jargon of ANT), of human practices. Even more so: "Agents are capable of constantly creating private money" (Callon 1999, 190)—but the reverse, i.e. that money creates agents or actors (or at least parts of their behavior) through its scripts, does not appear. In that sense his discourse is clearly praxeocentric and reproduces the praxeocentric fallacy. Latour seems to more strictly follow his own methodological premises, insofar he avoids any a priori asymmetry between money and other immutable mobiles. But in doing this he obviously doesn't follow the actors, who would surely underline the central role of money for their practices and the myriad ways in which money determines their situation (remember: no conference without money). In this way he erases the central role that money plays in relation to all other nonhuman actors.

So in fact we can find a *double repression of money in the discourse of ANT*: One concerning the relation between money and human actors and one concerning the relation between money and nonhuman actors (or to be more precise: that subset of nonhuman actors that Latour calls "immutable mobiles"). My critique does not mean that the theoretical and methodological interventions made by ANT are not useful for the study of money, especially when one tries to avoid the trap of determinisms. Moreover, I would argue, strictly adhering to the methodological principles of ANT would have avoided the double erasure of money—it seems to me that implicit political assumptions (connected to the nearly phobic avoidance of "critique"[35]) in Callon and Latour distort the possibilities of ANT.

A media theory of money to be developed can and should nevertheless draw on ANT and connect it to the theoretical resources available from media studies, philosophy, sociology, and economics. First of all, the idea of a symmetry between human and nonhuman actors should be taken seriously by granting the nonhuman actors agency. Money should be conceived neither a neutral tool nor as just one immutable mobile among others, but having a specific agency as a historically grown material, juridical, and governmental assemblage (or actor-network, if you like). Or to put it again in ANT-terms: money became a black box that now indeed operates as a determining force—this black-boxing process might explain why human actors normally take for granted that "money makes the world go round." This analysis might lead at the end to an—horribile dictum—informed critique of money; beyond a critique of the (perhaps "wrong") uses of money,[36] a political critique that may seem necessary today, more necessary than it ever was. It might in the end point to the possibilities of postmonetary societal structures, a discussion that has already begun: Rifkin (2014) argues for the possibility of "collaborative commons" replacing markets (see also, among many others, Siefkes 2016).

The conclusion is: When we search for media in markets, we might discover that not only the basic scripts of money (calculability, durability) changed with its changing medial form (mobility, stabilization through law, and copy protection, etc.) but also that new digital technologies might offer completely new forms that *even replace the basic scripts* (see Heidenreich and Heidenreich 2015, 104–36; Schröter 2017). Just designing new forms of currencies that, for example, cannot be accumulated because they lose value over time, might not be enough. It might be necessary to ask if there could be a co-constitution of new medial and social forms, which in the end moves beyond markets and its correlated and co-constituted medium: money. In the research project "Society after Money: Beginning a Dialogue,"[37] which the author started together with collaborators from sociology, (heterodox) economics, and theory of the commons, such questions are discussed. The contribution of media theory (following Seitter, Winkler, and others) to this endeavor is the insistence on the different layers of scripts, materiality, and "institutionality" of money as a medium—and the question how they can be described, differentiated, analyzed, and perhaps substituted or even made superfluous.

Such historical, empirical, and theoretical research is part of the program of "neocritical media studies" that I am proposing (see Schröter and Heilmann 2016). This program necessitates three steps: First, the rereading of texts on money, trying precisely to specify the contribution of media theory to the theory of money (in contrast to sociology, philosophy, and economics). The critical discussion of certain versions of ANT (not ANT as a whole) in this essay was part of this step. Second, a "monetary media archeology" has to be developed that rewrites the history of media in relation to money and its institutions, and thereby specifies the media history of money. And third, this should lead to a critical reevaluation of media history, part of which would be the rewriting of the media history of money. The entanglement and mutual co-constitution of specific material properties of money (as discussed in the section "Some General Remarks on Media Theory and Money"), law, and technologies of the police can be reconstructed historically. In case studies it could be shown how the coins made of silver or gold are connected to specific juridical and governmental regimes (see Caffentzis 1989). Nowadays, the emergence of bitcoins would be an interesting case (see Golumbia 2016).

Finally, when we search for media we might find out that changing media and correlated practices and institutions might put an end to forms that seemed to be natural—in our example: the formalization and digitization of society as a whole, what we could call "capital." We should at least develop theoretical tools that allow us a critical distance.

Notes

1 See Schüttpelz (2014). See also the very concise general introduction to praxeological theories in Reckwitz (2003).

2 Already in his texts from around 1857 or 1858, which were published much later as the *Grundrisse* (Marx 1993), Marx repeatedly called money a "medium of exchange." In 1892, Menger (1892, 239) also called money a "medium of exchange"—this shows, by the way, that the notion of "medium" has a history in the history of economic thought, which is often overlooked (e.g., in Hoffmann 2002, an otherwise impressive history of the notion of medium, the description of money as "medium of exchange" is not mentioned). Later in 1956, Parsons and Smelser (2005, 141) again used the definition of money as a medium of exchange. In 1964, Marshall McLuhan (2003, 179–96) called money a medium in his famous study *Understanding Media.*

3 To put it in somewhat simplified terms, since there is also the neoclassical-Keynesian synthesis and so on; see on its historical emergence Morgan and Rutherford (1998). On heterodox currents see Lee (2009).

4 That this holds true even in modern theories of market equilibrium was shown by Hahn (1987).

5 Although this would need a much more detailed analysis, one could mention the recent popularity of Nitzan and Bichler (2009) in so-called accelerationist discourse (see, e.g., Malik 2014). Although—of course—Nitzan and Bichler are themselves of Israeli origin and cannot be called "anti-Semitic" in any meaningful way, it remains problematic that their model of capital-as-power is built on (among other sources) Thorstein Veblen's difference between industry and business (Nitzan and Bichler 2009, 219–21), which seems to be analogous to the difference between productive and parasitic capital—an analogy that was already observed by Adorno (1955), who wrote on Veblen: "there is implicitly something like parasitic and productive" (1955, 95; my own translation of: "Es gibt bei ihm implizit etwas wie raffend und schaffend").

6 On symmetry see Latour (2005, 76): "ANT is not, I repeat is not, the establishment of some absurd 'symmetry between humans and non-humans.' To be symmetric, for us, simply means *not* to impose a priori some spurious *asymmetry* among human intentional action and a material world of causal relations." On intermediaries and mediators see Latour (2006, 37–42). The following statement by Latour especially indicates that mediators (in contrast

to intermediaries) are central for ANT: "The real difference between the two schools of thought becomes visible when the 'means' or 'tools' used in 'construction' are treated as mediators and not as mere intermediaries." (2006, 39)

7 One could debate if it is meaningful to discriminate high and low specificity, although digital code (as mentioned above) and money both seem to be of low specificity—and, not surprisingly, money has been compared to digital code (see Vief 1991). Some argue that the similarity of money and digital code regarding their universality may be the source of their conflict, at least as it is described in recent, neo-Marxian theories of economic crisis. See, e.g., Meretz (2007), who argues that digital data cannot easily be made to conform to the commodity form and therefore cannot easily be exchanged against money.

8 My translation. The German original is: "Siehe, die neuen Medien machen alles neu. Sie befreien uns von den schmutzigen Aspekten, die die traditionellen Medienströme kennzeichneten—von der Druckerschwärze, vom eucharistischen Blutstrom und auch von der anrüchigen Materialität des Pecunia-olet-Geldstroms. Die neuen Kommunikationsverhältnisse sind immateriell. Pixel sind weitgehend frei von Erdenschwere."

9 Ganßmann is quoting Parsons. On the problems of the notions of medium and code in Parsons and Luhmann, see Künzler (1987); see also Esposito (2008).

10 In this regard Winkler's position is close to chartalist theories of money that emphasize the constitutive role of the state for money (see Ingham 2005, xx–xxii). As one historical example for the problems of the forgery and manipulation of money, the so-called clipped coins problem in England, see Caffentzis (1989, 17–44).

11 The important role of these technologies is underlined by the fact that they themselves are juridically protected—an important mechanism of the entanglement of technology and law (see Senftleben 2010).

12 Krämer (2005, 88–89) underlines this: "One structural condition must be fulfilled by every embodiment of money. It has to have the form of an easily transportable, incorruptible piecework, that is: it has to be divisible into elements and thereby to be made discrete, so that it can be counted. Money is the stuff designed to be countable." (My translation of: "Eine strukturelle Bedingung allerdings muß jede Verkörperung des Geldes erfüllen. Sie muß die Gestalt eines einfach zu transportierenden, unverderblichen Stückwerks haben, also in Elemente teilbar, mithin diskretisierbar und abzählbar sein. Geld ist der Stoff, der auf seine Zählbarkeit hin entworfen ist.") Therefore, histories of digital media should be rewritten to include money.

13 Remember the quote from Hörisch (2004, 170) above, which suggests that money *becomes* more and more immaterial with the advent of "new media." The teleology is: first you have metal coins, then you have more "immaterial" banknotes, and then you have total immaterial electronic money. If money is digital, then one could argue that the advent of electronic money (administered by digital computing systems) is the coming-to-itself of money as such.

14 This is a complicated problem and only some hints can be provided. In times of crisis, calls often arise for a return to the gold standard, and most governments

today still hold remarkable reserves of gold. This shows that the (theoretically disputable) idea of intrinsically precious metals is still very much around (although gold nowadays is not used as money, but as a kind of allegedly stable commodity). In times of crisis, new forms of currency (like cigarettes) may also take the place of discredited money. These examples contradict a linear teleology of dematerialization.

15 See Marx (1992, 203): "The more the circulation metamorphoses of capital are only ideal, i.e. the closer the circulation time comes to zero, the more the capital functions, and the greater is its productivity and self-valorization." Clearly, Virilio's (1977) well-known diagnosis that modernity accelerates and accelerates is a direct effect of the circulation of capital and its tendency toward "zero time."

16 I cannot discuss the problems connected with the notion of performativity here; I discuss that at length in another article (see Schröter 2016). In that paper I also discuss the missing theory of crisis in Callon, a topic I do not mention here.

17 See Callon (in Barry and Slater 2002, 297): "Capitalism is an invention of anti-capitalists." In a way this statement isn't very helpful because it is obvious that a notion like "capitalism" is the result of a description that is based on a theoretical model (e.g. differentiation theorists like Niklas Luhmann wouldn't use it; he would speak of "functionally differentiated society").

18 The "experiments" seems to be Callon's term for so-called "real socialism" (see Callon 2007, 349).

19 Holm (2007, 239) is very explicit about that: "When the cyborg fish is in place, the most violent acts of dispossession against coastal communities have already been undertaken; the fisheries commons have already been closed; the heritage of the coastal people has already been parceled and laid out, ready for the auction. With the successful introduction of fisheries resource management, most of the organizational and institutional apparatus that could have served as a power base for those who want to resist ITQs has already been squashed." We read of "violence" through which the "commons" of the fishermen are closed and thereby the fishermen are "dispossessed." This is *exactly* the process of primitive accumulation as described by Marx. See also Callon (1998b, 24, 27) on "extending the spaces of calculation." See also Holm and Nielsen (2007) again on the "cyborg-fish."

20 The word *value* is sometimes used in Callon (1998b, 38, 50) in a vaguely moral sense: "values" that are opposed to the market.

21 The foundation of neoclassical theory on the principle of "methodological individualism" can be described as praxeocentric, insofar as the practices of principally isolatable actors (be they human and/or non-human) are the building blocks of the theoretical model. The relations of praxeocentrism to methodological individualism have to be discussed in more detail in future.

22 Callon often speaks of "economics" and of "economists" without specifying *which* economics he means. That suggests he simply accepts the reigning mainstream economics: that is, simply put, neoclassical theory (mentioned

e.g. in Callon 1998b, 22; see also Mirowski and Nik-Khah 2008, 96, 117). Callon refers to "standard economic theory" (1998c, 247) and marginalist analysis (1998c, 247–48), which is of course part of "standard" neoclassical theory. This already negates the conflict in economics between this mainstream and so-called heterodox economics (see Keen 2001; 2011 for a scathing critique of the neoclassical mainstream; see Lee 2009 on the history of heterodox economics). Callon (2005, 11) at least mentions "heterodox or even radical currents"—but prefers the orthodox one, presumably because it is dominant (in accordance to his theory of the performativity of economics). But by this he seems also to follow mainstream economics.

23 And it is a model, even when Callon (1999, 194) insists that ANT is not a theory.

24 This shows that money cannot easily be understood as a mere "sign" (on the sign-theories of money, see Hutter 1995).

25 See also Latour (1999, 289–90) on the Marxist critique of commodity fetishism. It has to be underlined that he is apparently familiar with a rather traditional version of Marxian theory: there is no indication that he is aware of newer theoretical approaches, e.g. the critique of value, although similar approaches exist in France. See Vincent (1997).

26 One example of such an investigation might be Preda (2006).

27 The situation is complicated by the fact that at least some forms of money in turn presuppose other immutable mobiles, such as security technology, etc. However, these in turn then presuppose money. It may be the case that the totality also has to be described as a kind of interdependent accretion (rather than as an addition), in which, however, money is ultimately, unlike other immutable mobiles, never dispensable—which is where the asymmetry would reside.

28 It is a separate question whether it always makes sense to talk of accumulating centers of calculation in relation to all other kinds of immutable mobiles. One gains the impression that the strongly centralized form of the French state has left its mark here.

29 Already in the title of Latour's famous study *Science in Action: How to Follow Scientists and Engineers through Society* (1987), it is made clear that "scientists" and "engineers" are the focus of observation. Schüttpelz (2009, 93) also talks of the "bureaucratic archive[s] of large, powerful organizations."

30 Although Latour insists on the visual aspects, it might be possible that immutable mobiles also have auditory, tactile, and other aspects. But perhaps the concept of the "immutable mobile" is somewhat oculocentric.

31 To be fair, Callon (2007, 350–51) also mentions in passing experimentation in cooperative forms.

32 See also Callon (1999, 181): "The most important is that ANT is based on no stable theory of the actor; in other words, it assumes the *radical indeterminacy* of the actor. For example, neither the actor's size nor its psychological make-up nor the motivations behind its actions are predetermined."

33 See Latour (1988, point 3.4.9) on the rejection of "nature" as origin. See also Latour (2005, 93): "In effect, what ANT was trying to modify was simply the use

of the whole critical repertoire by abandoning simultaneously the use of Nature and the use of Society, which had been invented to reveal 'behind' social phenomena what was 'really taking place.'"

34 See Potthast and Guggenheim (2015, 9) on the point that, for Latour, "the concept of network . . . refers to an ahistorical mode of connecting humans and non-humans."

35 See Latour (2005, 136–40) critically on "critique." See Callon regarding economics: "There are . . . positions we have to abandon. The first is the idea of critique of hard economists, which is intended to show them that [they] are wrong" (in Barry and Slater 2002, 301).

36 See Nelson (2012), who as a political activist explicitly criticizes the idea of money as a "neutral tool."

37 See http://nach-dem-geld.de. A publication in English is in preparation.

References

Adorno, Theodor W. 1955. "Veblens Angriff auf die Kultur." In *Prismen: Kulturkritik und Gesellschaft*, 82–111. Frankfurt am Main: Suhrkamp.

Akrich, Madeleine. 1992. "The De-Scription of Technical Objects." In *Shaping Technology/Building Society: Studies in Sociotechnical Change*, edited by Wiebe E. Bijker and John Law, 205–24. Cambridge, Mass.: MIT Press.

Barry, Andrew, and Don Slater. 2002. "Technology, Politics, and the Market: An Interview with Michel Callon." *Economy and Society* 31, no. 2: 285–306.

Bolz, Norbert. 1993. *Am Ende der Gutenberg-Galaxis: Die neuen Kommunikationsverhältnisse*. Munich: Fink.

Bulow, Jeremy. 1986. "An Economic Theory of Planned Obsolescence." *The Quarterly Journal of Economics* 101, no. 4: 729–49.

Caffentzis, Constantine George. 1989. *Clipped Coins, Abused Words, and Civil Government: John Locke's Philosophy of Money*. Brooklyn, N.Y.: Autonomedia.

Callon, Michel, ed. 1998a. *The Laws of the Markets*. Oxford: Blackwell.

Callon, Michel. 1998b. "Introduction." In *The Laws of the Markets*, edited by Michel Callon, 1–57. Oxford: Blackwell.

Callon, Michel. 1998c. "An Essay on Framing and Overflowing: Economic Externalities Revisited by Sociology." In *The Laws of the Markets*, edited by Michel Callon, 244–69. Oxford: Blackwell.

Callon, Michel. 1999. "Actor-Network Theory—The Market Test." In *Actor Network Theory and After*, edited by John Law and John Hassard, 181–95. Oxford: Blackwell.

Callon, Michel. 2005. "Why Virtualism Paves the Way to Political Impotence: Callon Replies to Miller." *Economic Sociology. European Electronic Newsletter* 6, no. 2: 3–20. Accessed March 30, 2016. http://econsoc.mpifg.de/archive/esfeb05.pdf.

Callon, Michel. 2007. "What Does It Mean to Say That Economics Is Performative?" In *Do Economists Make Markets? On the Performativity of Economics*, edited by Donald MacKenzie, Fabian Muniesa, and Lucia Siu, 311–57. Princeton, N.J.: Princeton University Press.

Daley, James. 2009. *The Book of Green Quotations.* Mineola, N.Y.: Dover.

Engster, Frank. 2014. *Das Geld als Maß, Mittel und Methode: Rechnen mit der Identität der Zeit.* Berlin: Neofelis.

Esposito, Elena. 2008. "Die normale Unwahrscheinlickeit der Medien: der Fall des Geldes." In *Was ist ein Medium?*, edited by Stefan Münker and Alexander Roesler, 112–30. Frankfurt am Main: Suhrkamp.

Fine, Ben. 2003. "Callonistics: A Disentanglement." *Economy and Society* 32, no. 3: 478–84.

Galloway, Alexander R. 2013. "The Poverty of Philosophy: Realism and Post-Fordism." *Critical Inquiry* 39, no. 2: 347–66.

Ganßmann, Heiner. 1988. "Money—a Symbolically Generalized Medium of Communication? On the Concept of Money in Recent Sociology." *Economy and Society* 17, no. 3: 285–316.

Gerloff, Wilhelm. 1952. *Geld und Gesellschaft: Versuch einer gesellschaftlichen Theorie des Geldes.* Frankfurt am Main: Klostermann.

Gillilland, Cora Lee C. 1975. *The Stone Money of Yap: A Numismatic Survey*. Washington, D.C.: Smithsonian Institution Press.

Golumbia, David. 2016. *The Politics of Bitcoin: Software as Right-Wing Extremism.* Minneapolis: University of Minnesota Press.

Hahn, Frank. 1987. "The Foundations of Monetary Theory." In *Monetary Theory and Economic Institutions: Proceedings of a Conference Held by the International Economic Association at Fiesole, Florence, Italy,* edited by Marcello de Cecco and Jean-Paul Fitoussi, 21–43. Hampshire, U.K.: Macmillan Press.

Heidenreich, Ralph, and Stefan Heidenreich. 2015. *Forderungen.* Berlin: Merve.

Hodgson, Geoffrey M. 2016. "Varieties of Capitalism: Some Philosophical and Historical Considerations." *Cambridge Journal of Economics* 40, no. 3: 941–60.

Hörisch, Jochen. 2004. *Gott. Geld, Medien: Studien zu den Medien, die die Welt im Innersten zusammenhalten.* Frankfurt am Main: Suhrkamp.

Hoffmann, Stefan. 2002. *Geschichte des Medienbegriffs.* Hamburg: Meiner.

Holm, Petter. 2007. "Which Way Is Up on Callon?" In *Do Economists Make Markets? On the Performativity of Economics,* edited by Donald McKenzie, Fabian Muniesa, and Lucia Siu, 225–43. Princeton, N.J.: Princeton University Press.

Holm, Petter, and Kåre Nolde Nielsen. 2007. "Framing Fish, Making Markets: The Construction of Individual Transferable Quotas." In *Market Devices,* edited by Michel Collon, Yuval Millo, and Fabian Muniesa, 173–95. Malden, Mass.: Blackwell.

Hughes, Nick, and Susie Lonie. 2007. "Mobile Money for the 'Unbanked': Turning Cellphones into 24-Hour Tellers in Kenya." *Innovations* 2, no. 1–2: 63–81.

Hutter, Michael. 1995. "Signum Non Olet." In *Rätsel Geld: Annäherungen aus ökonomischer, soziologischer und historischer Sicht,* edited by Waltraud Schelkle and Manfred Nitsch, 325–52. Marburg: Metropolis.

Ingham, Geoffrey, ed. 2005. *Concepts of Money.* Cheltenham and Northhampton, Mass.: Elgar.

Jappe, Anselm. 2005. *Die Abenteuer der Ware: Für eine neue Wertkritik*. Münster: Unrast.

Jones, Robert A. 1976. "The Origin and Development of Media of Exchange." *Journal of Political Economy* 84, no. 4: 757–75.

Keen, Steve. 2001. *Debunking Economics: The Naked Emperor of the Social Sciences.* Anandale: Pluto Press.
Keen, Steve. 2011. *Debunking Economics—Revised and Expanded Edition: The Naked Emperor Dethroned?* London: Zed Books.
Kittler, Friedrich. 1992. "There Is No Software." *Stanford Literature Review* 9, no. 1: 81–90.
Kittler, Friedrich. 1999. *Gramophone Film Typewriter.* Stanford, Calif.: Stanford University Press.
Koch, Robert. 2009. "'Alle Bäume auf dem Felde sollen mit den Händen klatschen': Medium und Metaphysik in der Akteur-Netzwerk-Theorie." *Sprache und Literatur* 40, no. 2: 4–20.
Kohl, Tobias. 2014. *Geld und Gesellschaft: Zu Entstehung, Funktionsweise und Kollaps von monetären Mechanismen, Zivilisation und sozialen Strukturen.* Marburg: Metropolis.
Krämer, Sybille. 2005. "Das Geld und die Null: Die Quantifizierung und die Visualisierung des Unsichtbaren in Kulturtechniken der frühen Neuzeit." In *Macht Wissen Wahrheit,* edited by Klaus W. Hempfer and Anita Traninger, 79–100. Freiburg and Berlin: Rombach.
Künzler, Jan. 1987. "Grundlagenprobleme der Theorie symbolisch generalisierter Kommunikationsmedien bei Niklas Luhmann." *Zeitschrift für Soziologie* 16, no. 5: 317–33.
Kurz, Robert. 2012. *Geld ohne Wert: Grundrisse zu einer Transformation der Kritik der politischen Ökonomie.* Berlin: Horlemann.
Larsen, Neil, et al., eds. 2014. *Marxism and the Critique of Value.* Chicago and Alberta: M-C-M'.
Latour, Bruno. 1986. "Visualisation and Cognition: Thinking with Eyes and Hands." In *Knowledge and Society: Studies in the Sociology of Culture Past and Present* 6:1–40.
Latour, Bruno. 1987. *Science in Action: How to Follow Scientists and Engineers through Society.* Cambridge, Mass.: Harvard University Press.
Latour, Bruno. 1988. "Irreductions." In *The Pasteurization of France,* 151–216. Cambridge, Mass.: Harvard University Press.
Latour, Bruno. 1999. *Pandora's Hope: Essays on the Reality of Science Studies.* Cambridge, Mass.: Harvard University Press.
Latour, Bruno. 2005. *Reassembling the Social: An Introduction to Actor-Network-Theory.* New York: Oxford University Press.
Law, John. 1987. "On the Social Explanation of Technical Change: The Case of the Portuguese Maritime Expansion." In *Technology and Culture* 28, no. 2: 227–52.
Lee, Frederic. 2009. *A History of Heterodox Economics: Challenging the Mainstream in the Twentieth Century.* New York: Routledge.
LeGoff, Jacques. 2012. *Money and the Middle Ages.* New York: Wiley.
Lotz, Christian. 2014. *The Capitalist Schema: Time, Money, and the Culture of Abstraction.* Lanham, Md.: Lexington Books.
Luhmann, Niklas. 1994. *Die Wirtschaft der Gesellschaft.* Frankfurt am Main: Suhrkamp.
Malik, Suhail. 2014. "The Ontology of Finance: Price, Power, and the Arkhéderivative." *Collapse: Philosophical Research and Development* 8:629–811.
Makin, Paul. 2011. "Regulatory Issues around Mobile Banking: New Initiatives to Bank

the Poor Are Straining the World's Financial Regulatory Systems." http://www.oecd.org/ict/4d/43631885.pdf. Accessed March 30, 2016.

Marx, Karl. 1990. *Capital. Volume I.* London: Penguin.

Marx, Karl. 1991. *Capital. Volume III.* London: Penguin.

Marx, Karl. 1992. *Capital. Volume II.* London: Penguin.

Marx, Karl. 1993. *Grundrisse.* London: Penguin.

McLuhan, Marshall. 2003. *Understanding Media: The Extensions of Man, Critical Edition.* Corte Madera, Calif.: Gingko Press.

Menger, Karl. 1892. "On the Origin of Money." *Economic Journal* 2, no. 6: 239–55.

Meretz, Stefan. 2007. "Der Kampf um die Warenform: Wie Knappheit bei Universalgütern hergestellt wird. " *Krisis—Beiträge zur Kritik der Warengesellschaft* 3, no. 1: 52–89.

Mill, John Stuart. 1936. *Principles of Political Economy with Some of Their Applications to Social Philosophy.* London: Longmans.

Mirowski, Philip, and Edward Nik-Khah. 2008. "Command Performance: Exploring What STS Thinks It Takes to Build a Market." In *Living in a Material World: Economic Sociology Meets Science and Technology Studies,* edited by Trevor Pinch and Richard Swedberg, 89–129. Cambridge, Mass.: MIT Press.

Morgan, Mary S., and Malcolm Rutherford. 1998. *From Interwar Pluralism to Postwar Neoclassicism.* Durham, N.C.: Duke University Press.

Nelson, Anitra. 2012. "Non-market Socialism: Life without Money—An Interview with Anitra Nelson." https://radicalnotes.com/2012/12/30/non-market-socialism-life-without-money-an-interview-with-anitra-nelson/. Accessed April 22, 2015.

Nitzan, Jonathan, and Shimshon Bichler. 2009. *Capital as Power: A Study of Order and Creorde.*. London: Routledge.

Orléan, André. 2014. *The Empire of Value: A New Foundation for Economics.* Cambridge, Mass.: MIT Press.

Pahl, Hanno. 2008. *Das Geld in der modernen Wirtschaft: Marx und Luhmann im Vergleich.* Frankfurt: Campus.

Parsons, Talcott, and Neil J. Smelser. 2005. *Economy and Society: A Study in the Integration of Economic and Social Theory.* New York: Routledge.

Pashukanis, Evgeny Bronislavovich. 2002. *The General Theory of Law and Marxism.* New Brunswick, N.J.: Transaction Publishers.

Polanyi, Karl. 2002. *The Great Transformation: The Political and Economic Origins of Our Time.* Boston, Mass.: Beacon Press.

Potthast, Jörg, and Michael Guggenheim. 2015. "Symmetrical Twins: On the Relationship Between Actor-Network Theory and the Sociology of Critical Capacities." http://research.gold.ac.uk/7001/1/Guggenheim_Potthast_symmetrical_twins.pdf. Accessed April 22, 2015.

Preda, Alex. 2006. "Socio-Technical Agency in Financial Markets: The Case of the Stock Ticker." *Social Studies of Science* 36, no. 5: 753–82.

Reckwitz, Andreas. 2003. "Grundelemente einer Theorie sozialer Praktiken: Eine sozialtheoretische Perspektive." *Zeitschrift für Soziologie* 32, no. 4: 282–301.

Rifkin, Jeremy. 2014. *The Zero Marginal Cost Society: The Internet of Things, the Collaborative Commons, and the Eclipse of Capitalism.* New York: Palgrave Macmillan.

Rotman, Brian. 1987. *Signifying Nothing: The Semiotics of Zero.* Stanford, Calif.: Stanford University Press.

Schröter, Jens. 2004. *Das Netz und die Virtuelle Realität: Zur Selbstprogrammierung der Gesellschaft durch die universelle Maschine.* Bielefeld: Transcript.

Schröter, Jens. 2015. "Das mediale Monopol des Staates und seine Verteidigungslinien." *Zeitschrift für Medien- und Kulturforschung* 6, no. 2: 13–24.

Schröter, Jens. 2016. "Performing the Economy, Digital Media, and Crisis: A Critique of Michel Callon." In *Performing the Digital: Performance Studies and Performances in Digital Cultures,* edited by Martina Leeker, Imanuel Schipper, and Timon Beyes, 247–78. Bielefeld: Transcript.

Schröter, Jens. 2017. "Der Markt, das implizite Wissen und die digitalen Medien." *Navigationen: Zeitschrift für Medien- und Kulturwissenschaften* 17, no. 2: 131–43.

Schröter, Jens, and Till Heilmann. 2016. "Zum Bonner Programm einer neo-kritischen Medienwissenschaft: Statt einer Einleitung." *Navigationen. Zeitschrift für Medien- und Kulturwissenschaften* 16, no. 2: 7–36.

Schüttpelz, Erhard. 2009. "Die medientechnischen Überlegenheit des Westens: Zur Geschichte und Geographie der *immutable mobiles* Bruno Latours." In *Mediengeographie: Theorie—Analyse—Diskussion,* edited by Jörg Döring and Tristan Thielmann, 67–110. Bielefeld: Transcript.

Schüttpelz, Erhard. 2013. "Elemente einer Akteur-Medien-Theorie." In *Akteur-Medien-Theorie,* edited by Tristan Thielmann and Erhard Schüttpelz, 9–70. Bielefeld: Transcript.

Schüttpelz, Erhard. 2014. "Connect and Divide: The Practice Turn in Media Studies." http://gepris.dfg.de/gepris/projekt/269878230. Accessed March 30, 2016.

Seitter, Walter. 2002. *Die Physik der Medien: Materialien, Apparate, Präsentierungen.* Weimar: VDG.

Senftleben, Martin. 2010. "The Answer to the Machine Revisited—Kopierschutz aus juristischer Sicht." In *Kulturen des Kopierschutzes I,* edited by Jens Schröter et al., 81-94. Siegen: universi.

Siefkes, Christian. 2016. "Freie Software und Commons: Digitale Ausnahme oder Beginn einer postkapitalistischen Produktionsweise?" *Navigationen: Zeitschrift für Medien- und Kulturwissenschaften* 16, no. 2: 37–54.

Vief, Bernhard. 1991. "Digitales Geld." In *Digitaler Schein: Ästhetik der elektronischen Medien,* edited by Florian Rötzer, 117–46. Frankfurt am Main: Suhrkamp.

Vincent, Jean Marie. 1997. "Marx l'obstiné." In *Marx aprés les marxismes,* edited by Michael Vakalouis and Jean Marie Vincent, 9–46. Paris: L'Harmattan.

Virilio, Paul. 1977. *Speed and Politics: An Essay on Dromology.* New York: Semiotext(e).

Winkler, Hartmut. 2004. *Diskursökonomie: Versuch über die innere Ökonomie der Medien.* Frankfurt am Main: Suhrkamp.

Wölbert, Christian. 2015. "Job-Maschinen: Wie Technik Probleme in Entwicklungsländern löst." *c't* 2:56–58.

Zelizer, Viviana. 1998. "The Proliferation of Social Currencies." In *The Laws of the Markets,* edited by Michel Callon, 58–68. Oxford: Blackwell.

Authors

Armin Beverungen is lecturer in media studies at the University of Siegen.

Philip Mirowski is Carl Koch Professor of Economics and the History and Philosophy of Science at the University of Notre Dame. He is author of *More Heat than Light: Economics as Social Physics, Physics as Nature's Economics, Machine Dreams: Economics Becomes a Cyborg Science, Science-Mart: Privatizing American Science, Never Let a Serious Crisis Go to Waste: How Neoliberalism Survived the Financial Meltdown,* and, with Edward Nik-Khah, *The Knowledge We Have Lost in Information: The History of Information in Modern Economics.*

Edward Nik-Khah is professor of economics at Roanoke College. He is the author, with Philip Mirowski, of *The Knowledge We Have Lost in Information: The History of Information in Modern Economics.*

Jens Schröter is professor of media studies at the University of Bonn. He is the author of *3D: History, Theory, and Aesthetics of the Transplane Image* as well as a number of books in German.